Relentless Mercy

The Life of Jonah and The God of Second Chances

Thank You...

To Mom and Dad for fighting for me even when I ran.

To Ryan for leading and loving me so well.
Wherever you are is home.

To our kids- Noah, Jackson, Seth, and Macy Jo.
You've taught me more lessons than anyone I know.
I love you bigly.

And finally,
To Jesus — who came after me time and again.
Thank you for making something beautiful out of my mess.
I love you with my whole heart.
All I have is yours.
Hosea 2:14-15

Contents

Introduction

I'll never forget the day one of my fellow stay-at-home-mom friends called and invited me to go to a group Bible study. I was 25 at the time and, though I'd been raised in church, I had never done a Bible study; in fact, if I'm being honest, even the thought of it seemed boring and tedious. In an effort to appear interested, I listened politely as she mentioned a few details about the location of the church, the type of study it was, and the free coffee and baking. All the while I sat there wondering how to let my friend down easily without letting on that I had zero desire to go to a women's Bible study. As she was nearing the end of her sales-pitch, almost as an after-thought, she said, "Oh, and there's free childcare." Why she didn't lead with this bit of holy information, I'm not sure. But there I was, hip-juggling my 11-month old, chasing my 3-year old, and facing the early stages of morning sickness from a very unexpected pregnancy. It was all I could do not to scream *YES, I'll go with you!* into the phone. I'm pretty sure I played it cool and acted interested in the Bible study, but on the inside, I was smiling and chanting "Free childcare! Free childcare!"

I wish it were something a little more spiritual that got me into the church that day but here's what I know to be true about God: he can use the everyday, ordinary things of life to get us in the door. I walked in the church for the childcare and walked out with a fire lit in my soul for studying Scripture. It completely changed my life. I began waking up early, staying up late and even using my kids precious nap times to sit with my Bible and study it. That was nine years ago and I am just as passionate about the study of God's Word to this day.

I don't know what your story is or how you ended up with this Bible study in your hands. But my prayer for you is that no matter what got you in the door, God would surprise and bless you through these next five weeks together. That, like me, he will light a fire in you for His Word.

Here are a few things you should know before we begin:

1.) This study was originally intended to be used as the "homework" component for a 6-week teaching on the book of Jonah. However, I have done my best to adapt it for those of you who either cannot make the class or live too far away to participate. If that's you, I want to say *welcome*. I wish I could see your face and hear your story and get to know you over a hot cup of coffee. This study can absolutely be done on your own or with a small group.
2.) I am primarily using the NIV Bible for this study. Feel free to use any translation you'd like, but if there is ever confusion about my translation sounding different than yours, this is likely the reason.
3.) Each week consists of four days of "homework". My hope is that you'd be able to complete each day in less than 30 minutes. There will be days that are much quicker and days where you may need to wrestle with some questions. Please know that my heart behind this study is not to give you one more thing to do every day. My hope is that as we make intentional space for the Lord, he will surprise us with fresh insights and some fun "ah-ha!" moments.

I have a deep desire to see the women of our generation become Biblically literate- not just to know the Word, but to love it and live it. So, join me as we pull up a chair and sit at the feet of Jesus. Let's lean in and learn from *him*.

elita

Day 1 - A Not-So-Happy Ending

I don't know about you, but I'm a sucker for a happy ending. It really doesn't matter if it's a movie or a book or a Facebook status update, I just love a good ending where everyone is happy and healthy and there is complete resolve. I do my best to steer clear of stories that leave lingering questions. I can't stand it when I'm left sitting in a movie theatre wondering about all the things that didn't happen: *What happened to that person? Did the wife live? Did that guy ever get his job back? And where did the dog go? Surely somebody saved it! WHAT HAPPENED*!? Call me intense, but I seriously have a hard time sleeping after an unresolved ending. And since we're on the subject, I have an embarrassing confession to make: I was a pre-teen when the movie *Titanic* came out. Girls, I saw it in the theatre no less than five times. I *wish* I were making this up. And I distinctly remember every time I watched it, I found myself hoping it would somehow end differently. (I mean, c'mon Rose. *There was room on the floating door for both you and Jack after the Titanic went down.* Ok, clearly, I still have issues with this movie.) But here's my point: things just don't sit well with me when stories are left in an open-ended way or, more specifically, in a way *I* don't want them to end. And this is probably a huge part of why the Lord led me to study Jonah. I tend to believe sometimes God likes to use things that rub us the wrong way to teach us a lesson or two.

Maybe it's been a while since you've read the book of Jonah, or maybe you never have, but I feel obligated to give you a major spoiler alert before we go any further: Jonah does not end with "happily ever after." There is no resolve. In fact, Jonah's short four-chapter story in the Bible ends with a series of questions.

Take a moment right now and flip to the very end of Jonah. According to the first part of Jonah 4:11, fill in the following blanks:

"And should I not _____ _____ for the great city of _____, in which there are more than a hundred and twenty thousand people who _____ tell their _____ hand from their _____...?"

One truth we are going to see on display in Jonah's life is God's concern for all people. This includes you, friend. He is concerned for you and about you. Those things taking up precious space in your heart and mind? He knows them. The past you can't outrun? He knows every detail of it. The difficult people you are struggling to love? He knows their names. God is interested in *all* that concerns you.

I've been around enough women in my life to know how hard we can be on ourselves. We have the ability to fixate on our mistakes and end our days with a running list of failures, thinking of what we could have done or said differently. Regardless of how we label it - as mom guilt, wife guilt, work guilt, or "I-ate-the-entire-bag-of-chips" guilt - it's real and *it.is.exhausting*! But if God doesn't hold shame over us, why do we insist on holding it over ourselves?

Still there are others of you, like me, who live with the reality of a troubled past that cannot be undone. We look at our bruises and assume we may be a little too damaged to be of any real use in God's

3

Kingdom. Struggling to believe God can make something beautiful out of our mistakes, we begin to accept the lie that our past defines our future.

Friends! Surely this is not the free life God meant for us to live. He is not making a list and presenting it to you as you lay down each night prompting you to feel overwhelmed with guilt. And lest you think I have it all figured out, you need to know right now that I am *far* from perfect. I've lost count of the number of times Ryan, my husband of 15 years, has come home to find me in a puddle of tears convinced I'm screwing up all four of our kids, mad at myself for not being an expert at budgeting, and sad I didn't get that workout in and it will be yet another failed swimsuit season. *Sheesh*. Why in the world are we so hard on ourselves? My desire for all of us is that we will begin to see, though Jonah's life, that there is hope for ours. That where we see our greatest mistakes, God sees potential for an even greater masterpiece.

Go ahead and read Jonah 1- 4.
(I promise it will be the only time I ask you to read the whole book in one sitting.)

Helpful hint*: *If you feel like you know the book of Jonah backwards and forwards, then I challenge you to change things up! Try choosing a different Bible translation so you can read it with fresh eyes. I highly recommend The Message paraphrase or the Amplified Bible, but feel free to choose whatever you'd like.*

As you read, give each chapter a title which seems to be the over-arching theme of that particular section. For example, chapter one could be called "Jonah runs from God" or "Jonah Hides." Whatever sticks out in the chapter to you, write it down below. We will return to these in the weeks to come:
Chapter 1: _____

Chapter 2: _____

Chapter 3: _____

Chapter 4: _____

Today was a lot of reading. One thing I can promise you is that spending time in the Word of God will *never* be a waste of your day. In fact, you are now empowered by the Holy Spirit and better equipped to face whatever comes. But don't just take my word for it.

Please look up 2 Timothy 3:16-17 and write those verses below:

Did you catch that last phrase? We will not just be partially equipped, friends. We will be fully, thoroughly, and completely equipped to do what God has in store for us to do *this* day. So, as you get up from your couch or that coffee shop or wherever it is you find yourself right now, I challenge you to look for ways the Lord will bring to life the Scriptures we've just read. I pray you'll be pleasantly surprised by the way God weaves the story of Jonah into our own lives over the next five weeks together. I can't wait. xo

Thoughts + Responses to today's study:
(At the end of each day's lesson I will give you this space to write down any thoughts that stick out to you or any responses you feel the Lord puts on your heart.)

Day 2 – What's in a Name?

A few years ago, at my kid's elementary school, the students performed a play based on the story of Jonah and the whale. The catch is that the setting of the play was the Old West. I know, it sounds funny. How can you recreate the story of Jonah with thick southern accents, cowboy boots and horses? But they did it. Really well, actually. And, to be honest, this Texas-born-and-raised-girl loved hearing sweet Canadian eight and nine-year-old kids put on their best southern accents. I felt right at home hearing every sentence end with "y'all." But more than that, it was while watching the play that night some years ago when the first seeds for this Bible study were planted firmly in my heart. How beautiful is our God that he not only allows the old to minister to the young, but the young can just as effectively minister to the old, often without even knowing it?

I'm so happy you're back today. I know we did a lot of reading yesterday and I appreciate you for it. Now that we have read the entire book and have a grasp on Jonah's story from start to finish, let's dig in a little deeper.

Please read Jonah 1:1-2.

We now have two of our main characters:

1. **The Lord**

     and

2. **_____, son of Amittai**

If you have access to a computer or smartphone, please look up the meaning of the name "Jonah" in Hebrew and record it here: _____

It is important to note that in the Old Testament a name was not only *identification*, but an *identity* as well.[1] In other words, it wasn't just a person's name, it was who they were. With this in mind, we will focus on the person of Jonah today.

Jonah's name, literally translated "dove," is connected to a bird species with some interesting behaviors. I am no bird-enthusiast, but after some basic research, I learned doves have "powerful and fast flight."[2] It has the ability to fly like an arrow which knows it's trajectory - full of speed and accuracy. Not only are they flighty, but doves will abandon both their nest and eggs if they feel threatened and will look for a new nesting place.[3]

Underline anything about the behavior of doves that sticks out to you in the above paragraph.

King David once prayed the following prayer:

> *"Oh, that I had the wings of a dove!*
> *I would fly away and be at rest.*
> *I would flee far away*
> *and stay in the desert;*
> *I would hurry to my place of shelter,*
> *far from the tempest and storm."*
> Psalm 55:6-8

Circle any words or phrases in those verses that sheds more light on the behavior of doves.

It's interesting, isn't it? Jonah's name coincides with a bird known for speed, accuracy, and the ability to abandon everything else when threatened.

Read Jonah 1:3 and in the space below write down any connections between the meaning of Jonah's name ("dove") and the behavior he displays in this verse.

I wonder, do you happen to know what *your name* means? If so, please jot it down in the blank space below. If you don't know what your name means, go ahead and look it up and record it below.

Record any ways you feel your life has echoed the meaning of your name so far. Or perhaps the opposite is true and you feel your life doesn't identify at all with the name you were given. If so, explain and be prepared to discuss in class.

We don't know much about Jonah. We don't know how he grew up or what his parents were like. Was he an only child or was he the classic middle child, forever trying to keep the peace? Did he ever get married? Was he a father? These are questions we just can't answer this side of Heaven. But here is what we do know from the three short verses we looked at today: Jonah did the very thing his name suggested he would do: he fled. The Bible doesn't say he prayed about it or thought about it or consulted others about it. It simply says God told him to go one way and clear as day, Jonah went the other way.

I wonder if any of us, like Jonah, feel tethered to an identity we can't escape from; if any of us feel stuck thinking "that's not who I want to be, but it's just who I am." Friend, please hear this today: Satan will try to cheat you into thinking that because that's who you've always been, that's who you'll always be. But be reminded right now that if you are a Christian, then *the moment* you accepted Jesus Christ as your Lord and Savior, HIS name got plastered all over you. YOU, daughter of the King, are covered by the blood of Jesus. It's in HIS name alone that your past is forgiven and your future is secure. Your identity is no longer defined by who you were; it is now covered by who Jesus is. Both your name and mine, no matter how beautiful or ugly their meaning, pale in comparison to the redemptive, healing name of Jesus Christ. No matter your past, no matter what you are drawn to, entangled in, or afraid to let go of – Jesus paid the price and his blood has the power to change the trajectory of your entire life.

As we come to a close on day two, I can think of no better way to end than with the following portion of

Scripture:

"But Moses protested, "If I go to the people of Israel and tell them, 'The God of your ancestors has sent me to you,' they won't believe me. They will ask, 'Which god are you talking about? What is his name?' Then what should I tell them?" God replied, "I AM THE ONE WHO ALWAYS IS. Just tell them, 'I AM has sent me to you.'" God also said, "Tell them, 'The Lord, the God of your ancestors — the God of Abraham, the God of Isaac, and the God of Jacob — has sent me to you.' This will be my name forever; it has always been my name, and it will be used throughout all generations." Exodus 3:13-15

HIS NAME, friend. It's more than enough to cover us all.

Thoughts + Responses to today's study:

Day 3- *A History Lesson*

I tend to think that when it comes to formal education, there are two types of people: those who like school and those who do not. I fall squarely into the first category. I come by my love of learning honestly from my dad. Although he has both his master's and PhD, he often jokes he could happily sit in a classroom for the rest of his life. Now, I'm not sure I love school quite at this level, but as long as math and science aren't involved, I am a keen student.

I hope, regardless of your feelings about school, you'll stick with me today and tomorrow because we are going to do a little history lesson. I promise to make it as painless as possible, but I can't lie: sometimes the best lessons are learned only after we've put in a little bit of work. In order for us to be good students of the Word, and in our case the book of Jonah, it is necessary to learn about the culture and the time in which this story is taking place. So let's rewind our clocks by several thousand years and settle in about 800-750 BC.

The first time Jonah's name appears in the Bible is in 2 Kings 14:25. **Please turn to this passage and read it.**

According to 2 Kings, Jonah was known as "the _____ from Gath Hepher."

Glancing back at Jonah 1:1, how does his title in the book of Jonah differ from his title in 2 Kings?

In your own words, what is a prophet?

If you've been in church long enough, you'll know there are a lot of opinions and thoughts surrounding the idea of "the prophetic." Let me put your mind at ease and tell you right now that we are not even going to attempt to scratch the surface on this. But I do want to offer up a little bit of free advice: no matter what side of the issue you find yourself on - whether you love the prophetic or you have unanswered questions about it or maybe you've actually been deeply hurt by a mishandling of it- let's remember that we all sit at the same table, friends. We can disagree and still treat each other with dignity. We can, and should, have hard conversations, but I beg you to remember that the world is watching. Even when we think they aren't. Even when we forget. They watch how Christians handle conflict and whether we respond with grace or react with criticism. In a social media driven world where anyone can have a platform, let us not forget the beauty that comes from keeping our mouths closed and our ears open.

Keeping this in mind, briefly consider what your experience has been with prophecy. Would you say you are open to it or that you have a hard time with it? Please answer as honestly as possible.

Regardless of our personal opinions on it, prophecy is actually something the Lord introduced. He originally gave it as a gift to his chosen, yet often stubborn, people, the Israelites. *Stick with me here because I promise this will be good.* **Please turn to Deuteronomy chapter 18** and save this spot while I share a little background information about what we are getting ready to read.

We have just opened up our Bibles to find Moses, at 120 years old, standing before the entire assembly of Israel for his last time. Here we have a man who felt unqualified and unequipped, but God chose him anyway (Exodus 4:10-13). We have a man who allowed God to use him, despite his insecurities, to deliver over a million people from slavery (Exodus 12:37). We have a man who then led these fickle people for 40 years - he led them through the wandering and the wonders. He was there for it all- every miracle and every milestone. Moses is a man who exhausted himself and fought for the people standing in front of him. And this, right here in Deuteronomy, is his last time to ever address his people and what's more is that *he knows it*. Pause with me here and consider the emotion and the weight of what we are reading. I don't know about you, but if I knew I had one last chance to instruct my kids before the Lord took me home, there are some things I'd want to say. Do you know what I mean? There are some lessons I'd want to teach them, some "when this happens, do this" instructions.

If you had to say goodbye to your family today, what is one thing you would want to say to them? One final thing you'd want them to remember?

Now that we are nice and emotional, let us consider that the exercise we have just done is exactly what we find Moses doing in Deuteronomy. The entire book is a record of his final address to the Israelites. He has spent the first part of Deuteronomy reminding them of where they've come from and reviewing the many new laws, regulations, & ways of life the Lord had instituted. These included the Ten Commandments, instructions for Passover and Festival celebrations, tithes and offerings, clean and unclean animals, and a dizzying amount more. But suddenly in the midst of all this, we see Moses reveal God's gift of a prophet before the entire assembly of Israel.

Please read Deuteronomy 18:15-22 and answer the following questions:

-Why did the Lord promise to send a prophet to the Israelites? (v.16)

-At the risk of over-emphasizing the point, who was it that desired "not to hear again the voice of the Lord"?

Turn to Exodus 20:18-21 and read the original account between the Israelites and God.

The people of Israel asked for a mediator – someone to talk to them on God's behalf. And God was faithful to his promise. He sent men and women over the next several generations who spoke for him to his people: Joshua, Deborah, Micah, Elijah, Isaiah, Amos, and many, many more. And in the midst of all these prophets sent by God, we find Jonah. A prophet, called by God, who ran for his life. Do you wonder why? I sure do. But we will get to that tomorrow.

As we close today, I want to circle back around to a Scripture we've just read. Please go back and take a look at Exodus 20:21 and write it below:

Something stirs deep in my soul when I read that. Oh friend, I earnestly pray we will be like Moses. That we will be women who are not content with remaining at a distance to where God is calling us. That we would have the guts and the grit to press through the crowd, even if everyone else stays back in fear. That as we set our eyes on the prize of His beautiful presence, we would boldly come before him, not settling for anything other than an unveiled, unhindered relationship with him. There will be times we will have to push through our natural feelings, fears and frustrations, and refuse to let "at a distance" be good enough. Like the Israelites, God is inviting all of us in. Not just some of us. And *that* is beautiful news.

You are so loved. See you tomorrow.

Thoughts + Responses to today's study:

Day 4- *But Jonah*

What was your favorite board game as a kid? Most of my friends liked Monopoly but that was a little too sophisticated, and a little too time-consuming, for me. I loved playing Clue. Anybody else? I liked collecting evidence and trying to figure out the mystery in front of me. And I think studying Scripture can be a little like playing Clue sometimes, can't it? We read it, we ask the Lord questions, and then we try to find the answer, or at the very least, a clue. That's exactly what we are doing today. Together we will be prayerfully searching the text for clues which point us in the right direction. I deeply desire to handle God's word well- I don't ever want to deviate from what the Holy Spirit has already masterfully penned. But sometimes it takes a little work on our end to connect the dots sitting right in front of us.

Yesterday we narrowed in on Jonah's role as a prophet. Today we will go a step further in our history lesson and consider the reasons why Jonah may have run away from God's call to Nineveh. But first, a little geography lesson:

Read Jonah 1:1-3.
As you read, find the three cities that are named and circle them on the map located in the back of this homework guide (page 75).

If you'll remember from our reading yesterday, according to 2 Kings 14:25 Jonah was from a town in Israel called Gath Hepher. We can reasonably assume he was living there at the time God called him to go to Nineveh. So let's go ahead and **circle Gath Hepher as well.**

Now draw an arrow from Gath Hepher to Nineveh and label it "The Mission."

Next, draw an arrow from Gath Hepher to Joppa, and then another arrow from Joppa to Tarshish. Above these arrows you can label it, "The Escape."

If you're anything like me, sometimes a visual does much more than an explanation ever could. Hopefully by drawing it out you can see for yourself how directionally opposite Jonah attempted to go. He didn't just want to get a little out of the way. He wanted to get as far away as he possibly could.

In your own words, what did God tell Jonah to do in Jonah 1:2?

Please handwrite the first sentence of Jonah 1:3:

Underline the first two words of that sentence.

No matter what translation of the Bible you are using, those first two words should be the same for all of us: "But Jonah."

Let's pause here for a moment and consider something lest we cast unfair judgement on Jonah: have you ever felt the Lord prompt you to do something and you did something else instead? Please tell me I'm not alone in this. I can think of several times over the course of my born-again life where I sensed the Lord giving me a specific instruction and instead I had a "But Elita" moment. A moment where, if someone were writing my biography they might say, "The Lord instructed her to_____, *but Elita* got up and went in the opposite direction." **Can you think of a specific time, perhaps even recently, where you had a moment like this? Please jot it down below:**

I don't bring this up in order for us to re-hash old mistakes and feel bad all over again. Satan would love nothing more than to cast a shadow over God's forgiveness with our self-condemnation. But as we grow into a mature faith, we must be able to walk in the tension of learning from our wounds without bleeding from them for the rest of our lives. Let's not forget there is value in looking in our rear-view mirrors and learning from our mistakes so that the next time the Lord speaks, our ears are open, our hearts are ready, and our feet are willing to move wherever and whenever he says to go.

Do you wonder why Jonah went "in the opposite direction to get away from the Lord?" I sure do. **Write at least one or two reasons why you think Jonah might have run from God.**

Do you remember I said we are connecting dots today? Please keep this in mind as we continue our study. We are going to narrow in on **three possible reasons** Jonah may have run from God's call to Nineveh:

Reason #1: Prophets only dealt with Israel

This should be fresh on our minds from yesterday so we won't camp here long.
According to the verses we looked at in Deuteronomy 18:15-22, God created prophets to speak on his behalf to whom? _____

Prophets were originally created and intended to speak to Israel, God's chosen people. So, imagine Jonah's surprise when, out of the blue, God tells him to do something completely unheard of, completely unprecedented: go give a word to a nation that isn't Israel. And as we will see in our next point, it was not just any nation – it was Nineveh, the mighty and famous capital of the heathen Empire of Assyria, a constant enemy of Israel.[4] And any enemy of Israel was an enemy of Jonah.

Reason #2: Nineveh was an enemy of Israel

My husband builds and renovates homes for a living. He often says something I believe is relevant to what we are getting ready to look at: foundations matter. It matters with houses and it matters with kingdoms.

Please read Genesis 10:8-12 and fill in the following blanks as you read:

"Cush was the father of _____, who became a _____ warrior on the earth. He was a _____ hunter before the Lord; that is why it is said, 'Like Nimrod, a _____hunter before the Lord.'

The Hebrew word for "mighty" that is used here means "*powerful*; by implication *a warrior, tyrant*."[5] If this interpretation is correct, it follows that Nimrod's power and success, including the planting of cities like Nineveh, were founded under a *violent, tyrannical rule*.[6]

Foundations. They really do matter. It stands to reason if something is built on violence, then violence will be its way.

According to verse eleven, Nimrod "went to Assyria, where he built _____."

Located in modern-day Iraq, Nineveh grew to become a thriving city in the kingdom of Assyria. In fact, Nineveh became Assyria's most important center, and eventually its capital, because of its strategic location.[7] Like all Assyrians, the Ninevites were a military people. Obsessed with wealth and the worship of many false gods, they made a name for themselves among other people groups as being especially cruel. The Ninevites themselves recorded their own brutality on the walls of their palace. Found among the ruins of Nineveh are wall sculptures, called "reliefs", that "depict naked Judaeans impaled on poles, siege ramps built by Judaean slaves (who were forced to attack their own kinsmen). Assyrian reliefs depict the cruelty with which Assyrian forces treated defeated people groups. Assyrians commonly impaled, dismembered, decapitated, and disfigured defeated peoples. The Assyrians were ruthless and harsh overlords."[8]

In the century before Jonah comes onto the scene, two of the Kings of Assyria gave written records bragging about their own cruelty. These records, which were found in the ruins of Nineveh, allow us to move from a birds-eye view of the evil in Assyria and focus specifically on the climate of Nineveh shortly before Jonah's call to go there. King Ashurnasirpal II (883-859 BC) tells us, "I captured soldiers alive [and] erected [them] on stakes before their cities."[9] And his son, King Shalmanaser III (859-824 BC), wrote: "I filled the wide plain with the corpses of warriors… These [rebels] I impaled on stakes…A pyramid (pillar) of heads I erected in front of the city."[10]

And finally, the Bible describes Nineveh in this way: "Woe to the city of blood, full of lies, full of plunder, never without victims" Nahum 3:1

I admit that while these accounts are not easy to read, I am trying to get us uncomfortable. Something should stir in us when we read this. Some sense of justice should rise to the surface. And hopefully a new level of understanding has taken root as to why Jonah and the people of Israel held Nineveh in such contempt.

Did you learn anything about Nineveh/Assyria which helped you to understand why Jonah wouldn't have wanted to go to them and preach a message of repentance?

Reason #3: Jonah knew God might change his mind

Now that we know Nineveh a little better, we may be able to understand why Jonah wouldn't want God to change his mind regarding this corrupt city. But as evil as Nineveh was, Jonah knew that God was even more abundant in mercy.

Please read Jonah 4:2 and then Exodus 34:6. Write down any words that appear in both verses which describe the characteristics of God.

Because he would have been well-versed in the Scriptures, Jonah's description was a clear reference to Exodus. He knew God reserves the right to forgive and to have compassion. He knew there was a very real possibility if his enemies repented, God would relent.

I told you in our first class that we were going to ask the Lord for a fresh dose of mercy. Not on us. But from us. We are asking him to help us begin loving those hard people in our lives a little better. That we would begin to see them with fresh eyes and our hearts would become raw with grace towards those who hurt us and offend us. I'm going to leave some space below for you to **write down the initials of those difficult people in your life you are having a hard time with right now**. We will keep these names before us throughout this study as we ask God to help us have a shift in perspective towards them.

And so we will begin to wrestle here with something Jonah also had to wrestle with: God's love and God's mercy extends to all people; even to those who have wronged us, abused us, manipulated us, hurt us, used us, and to those we just wish would get what they deserve. Indeed, his compassion extends even towards you and me.

"At one time we too were foolish, disobedient, deceived and enslaved by all kinds of passions and pleasures. We lived in malice and envy, being hated and hating one another. But when the kindness and love of God our Savior appeared, he saved us, not because of righteous things we had done, but because of his mercy." Titus 3:3-5

You have done so well this week, my friends. See you in class. xo

Thoughts + Responses to today's study:

Day 1 – *Uncharted Waters*

Welcome back, ladies! As we head into week two of our study, I want you to know how greatly I applaud your willingness to show up and get into the Word. Many of us are battling with work schedules, newborn schedules, school schedules, and let's face it...just the busy-ness of L.I.F.E. I know we don't study the Bible for man's approval, but friend – I am so very proud of you. Because this digging and sowing you are doing will surely reap a great reward.

Last week we focused on the history of Jonah. It was an important foundation to lay in order for us to understand the rest of the book. This week we will confront a fundamental fact about our God-given identity; it's a truth we must remember in those moments when guilt and shame seek to drown out every other voice.

Look up Romans 11:29 and fill in the following blanks:

"for God's _____ and God's _____ are _____."

It was true for Jonah, and it is true for us. When God called Jonah, it was not by accident. When Jonah ran, he did not outrun God. When Jonah said no, God took steps to recover him.

Please read Jonah 1:4-17.

According to these verses, God took 2 steps to recover Jonah. He sent:

#1: a violent _____ (v. 4)

#2: a huge _____ (v.17).

My parents and I were once caught in a storm while with some friends on their small speedboat. We were in the middle of Lake Conroe, just outside of our hometown of Houston, Texas, when big, black clouds suddenly rolled in, blocking sun and sky. Almost immediately the thick southern heat began to disperse as the wind picked up. It was amazing how quickly the storm was upon us and how high the waves grew. As the nose of the boat plunged down over each wave and then climbed back up again for the next swell, the water splashed up and over the sides and soaked us through. We were in no real danger – in fact my friend and I sat at the nose of the boat as it tossed us around, laughing our teenage heads off thinking how much fun the whole thing was. The adults were in the back trying to hold down lunch.

What about you? Have you ever been on a ship or a boat that was caught in a storm? If so, describe the emotions you experienced.

Jonah thought himself safe and on his way. **He felt so secure, in fact, that according to verse five, Jonah had gone below deck and we find him doing what?**

He wasn't just resting his eyes. He was in a deep sleep. Some commentaries even suggest Jonah had spent so much time, energy, and focus on executing his escape plan, that this may have been his first time to experience heavy sleep since God first called him to Nineveh. Sin does this to us, by the way- it lures us in and makes us feel safe; it numbs our senses and dumbs us down. We become painfully unaware of the danger around us. I love the way commentator Matthew Henry describes this scene of Jonah asleep on the ship:

> *"Sin is of a stupifying nature, and we are concerned to take heed lest at any time our hearts be hardened by the deceitfulness of it. It is the policy of Satan, when by his temptations he has drawn men from God and their duty, to rock them asleep in carnal security, that they may not be sensible of their misery and danger. It concerns us all to watch therefore."[11]*

…Watch therefore. It's a warning for all of us. Sin gives us a false-sense of peace when in reality, the whole boat is about to go down. But here's the beautiful message we find written throughout the pages of Jonah, and indeed, throughout the whole Bible: God is in the business of recovering us. Even those of us who had no idea we needed rescuing in the first place.

Please read the following passages of Scripture. In each instance, write down the lengths to which God goes to retrieve his children. You can be as brief or as detailed as you would like:

Luke 15:4-6

Acts 8:26-39

Acts 9:1-22

Exodus 3:1-6

Romans 5:6-11

He leaves the ninety-nine. He sends complete strangers to share the good news about Jesus. He does miracles in the middle of roads to change murderers into walking testimonies of grace. He speaks on mountain sides to people who weren't even looking for him. He sent his own son to die for you and for me –to retrieve us once and for all time.

Take a moment now and reflect on your life thus far. In what ways has God rescued you?

Sometimes the way God rescues us isn't pretty and it isn't subtle. When we refuse to humble ourselves, God will do it for us. That's how part of my story goes, anyway. I was asleep on my "boat" thinking I was safe. But God sent a storm after me. He woke me up with the gentility of someone throwing a bucket of ice on an unsuspecting sleeper. Like Jonah, he sent the wind after me to fetch me back again to God and to his plans for me here on this earth. I can say as confidently as someone who was ever lost but now is found, that "it is a great mercy to be reclaimed and called home when we go astray, though it be by a storm."[12] Some people need the storms to get their attention.

We all have seasons where we just feel like we've missed the boat. No pun intended, but it's so appropriate, isn't it? Sometimes we feel like we are just too far gone. I pray today you were reminded of the depths God will go to retrieve *you*. Romans 11:29 in the Amplified Bible says it this way:

"For the gifts and the calling of God are irrevocable [for He does not withdraw what He has given, nor does He change His mind about those to whom He gives His grace or to whom He sends His call]."

Take a moment and look up the definition for the word "irrevocable." Write down your findings here:

Irrevocable may just be one of my new favorite words to describe the Lord. It means binding, final, unchangeable, permanent, immutable, fixed, conclusive. Oh friend, God's gifts *to* you and God's call *on* you are sealed. God has a specific plan for YOU. He has a detailed purpose for YOU. He has not changed his mind about you.

Fill in the following blanks with your name and be reminded…

When God called_____, it was not by accident.

When _____ messed up, she did not destroy God's plan for her life.

God's gift to _____ and God's call on _____ are irrevocable and sealed.

If you are able and willing to, I encourage you to read those statements out loud. Declare the truth of it over your soul. Let the Devil hear you know to whom you belong and, no matter your past, your future is secure in Christ. Let him know that if, like Jonah, you've been lured into a false sense of security, you are now awake and alert to the promises of God.

Unfamiliar and uncharted waters. Oh friend, there is no better place to learn to trust God.

Thoughts + Responses to today's study:

Day 2 – *Saved by a Storm*

When my husband and I were living in Mobile, Alabama, we became very well acquainted with hurricane season. The local news stations, and even The Weather Channel, would always keep us on edge with their worst-case-scenario predictions. They'd tell us to board up our windows, evacuate, and buy a generator. It was well-meaning, of course, but we rarely did any of those things because the storm would usually lose its strength or shift its path. But that all changed in September of 2004. Hurricane Ivan formed into a category 5 storm with 163mph winds and it was headed straight for our hometown; it never wavered in its trajectory. Our city went nuts. Most people, including us, decided to board up and head north. While driving on the 10-hour evacuation route to Nashville, I got a call from a friend. Her sweet husband, who was not at all worried about the hurricane, was determined they should stay and ride it out; they would not be evacuating. She called me from her closet, crying and distressed, and admitted she was afraid for her life. By this time in our relationship, my friend and I had already had ample conversations about faith and God and life; even so, I knew this was a unique moment before us. Now, please hear me when I say I would have loved to "officially" share Jesus with her under different circumstances, but I felt this was an appointed opportunity before us and so I took it. I was honored and humbled to be able to pray with my friend, right then and there, as she confessed her faith in Jesus. When we finished praying, even though I couldn't see her, I could hear the shift in her voice. She spoke with a confidence and a trust that hadn't been there only moments before. Gone were the anxious tears and the fear. It was breathtaking. That hurricane, with its violent winds, floods and catastrophic damage, was the instrument God used to invite my friend into his family and save her soul.

Yesterday we read Jonah 1:4-16. Please read it again to refresh your memory.

Today we will spend our time with the sailors. These men are, hands down, one of my favorite parts of Jonah's story. While Jonah may have been ignorant to the storm surrounding him, the sailors were hyper-aware of what they were up against. According to some scholars, these sailors were likely Phoenicians. If this is the case, the storm must have been especially terrifying because the Phoenicians were legendary for their seamanship and navigating skills.[13] Sailing was their occupation and they had likely been through many rough, stormy waters before. But something about this storm was different; it was enough to strike fear in them.

According to Jonah 1:5, the sailors did two things after the storm came upon them. What were they?

1._____

2._____

First, they prayed and then they acted.

We would do well to learn this simple lesson from the heathen sailors: start on your knees. While they were certainly not praying to the right god, the fact that they had enough instinct to pray first and then act speaks volumes. Often times we reverse the two, don't we? Like Jonah, we try to do things our way *first* and then we pray. It usually doesn't end up going very well, does it? But it's not just us. The Bible is full of men and women who were far from perfect.

Read Genesis 15:3-6 and answer the following questions:

What did God promise Abram?

According to verse 6, what was Abram's response to this promise?

Now fast-forward a chapter and read Genesis 16:1-4.

What steps did Sarai and Abram take in order to have a baby? Is there any evidence they consulted with or asked God first?

And so, a baby boy named Ishmael was conceived and then born nine months later. Sometimes, when we make things happen on our own, they really can give us temporary satisfaction. Let's not be so spiritual we can't admit this. Satan lures us in by promising us the joy of quick results without the work. But the good news is that God's plans are never thwarted by our mistakes. 14 years after Ishmael's birth, God was faithful to his covenant with Abram and gave him the promised son, Isaac, from whom the nation of Israel was born.

Turn and read Genesis 21:1-3. Complete the following sentence according to verse one:

"and the Lord did for Sarah _____ _____ _____ _____."

God is faithful. It is who he is. But make no mistake: Abram and Sarai did not get away with their disobedience. In fact, the consequences of their actions would affect generations.

Read Genesis 25:17-18 and record the last sentence here:

Psalm 83:4-6 gives us a glance into the future, hundreds of years after Abram's death. Please read it and record how the Ishmaelites interacted with the Israelites, who are the descendants of Isaac:

Abram managed to create a whole lineage of people who would become one of the greatest enemies of Israel, God's chosen people. Disobedience will always cost us something. When we refuse to wait on the promises of God (Isaac) we will always give birth to a human-designed counterfeit (Ishmael).

Can you think of a time when you acted first before praying? What did it cost you?

Don't allow yourself to get swallowed up in condemnation, friend. The aim of this study is not to focus on what sin has costs us, but rather to magnify how God has redeemed and restored us.

Look back to the beginning of our lesson if you need to, but please recall: **after the sailors on Jonah's boat prayed to their gods, what did they do?**

According to verse five, they did this in order to "_____ _____ _____."

After the sailors prayed to their gods, they threw the cargo into the sea to lighten the ship. They instinctively knew that the lighter the ship, the more likely they'd be to survive. Friend, when a storm arrives on your doorstep and catches you by surprise, there may be times when you need to lighten your load in order to focus on what really matters. I can think of times when it felt like my life might capsize under the weight I was carrying. It's in those seasons when it is not only ok, but it is necessary, to get rid of some excess; to put aside tasks we'd normally be able to manage and say no to some things that are usually routine.

According to Hebrews 12:1, we are to throw off what?

If we were to sit and think about some things cluttering our lives, I'd be willing to bet we could all come up with at least a few things which are distracting us from what really matters. Maybe it's social media or that reality show that keeps you coming back season after season, even though we all know it's border-line shameful. Maybe it's an unhealthy relationship or a dangerous obsession with diet and exercise. Here is what I want to suggest to you, my friend: there may be times in our lives when we are called to throw off some things we simply don't want to throw off. Some things we enjoy. Some things that perhaps even used to be beneficial in our lives. But, like the sailors on Jonah's boat realized, sometimes there are things in our lives that, though they may have once helped us, can have the ability to hinder us from moving forward.

Use your imagination: what kind of things do you think the sailors had to throw overboard?

The sailors likely had to throw out supplies they'd needed – cargo they were being paid to transport and perhaps even their supply of fresh water and food. In an instant, those things that had once been so important paled in comparison to simply staying alive.

Interestingly, the sailors quickly recognized there was some other "weight" on the ship they couldn't pinpoint.

According to Jonah 1:7, the sailors wanted to cast lots to find out what exactly?

The King James Version says it this way: "let us cast lots, that we may know for whose cause this *evil* is upon us." When the lot fell on Jonah and they realized he was the dead weight on their ship, they subjected him to a mini-interrogation.

Re-read Jonah 1:8. How many questions did they ask Jonah? _____

This line of questioning shows they had NO idea who they'd let onto their boat. And I wonder about us. Do we know who or what we've let into our "boats"? We might be looking at the wind and the water wondering when the storm is going to pass when in fact there might be something in our *very own lives* that needs uncovering, dealing with, and throwing out of "our boat." Are there things threatening to sink your marriage? Your family? Your finances? Your friendships? It may not be anything bad, mind you. The kind-hearted sailors did everything they could so they wouldn't have to throw Jonah overboard; they were determined they would not be responsible for his death. But God required this of them: to throw over the thing that was causing their ship to sink, not just to save them, but to save Jonah as well.

Take a moment with the Lord right now. I encourage you to ask him if there's anything in your life that's dead weight; anything that is tethered to you that needs to be cut loose. Perhaps it isn't just for your sake, but for someone else's, as well. If you sense God has put something on your heart, and if are willing to, you can write that down below. Sometimes putting it on paper helps us feel more accountable to do something about it.

Look again at Jonah 1:15-16.

I cannot help but smile at the fact that God used Jonah's willful disobedience to expand his kingdom. A whole ship full of men had their entire lives rerouted and set on a new course. These sailors, who would have otherwise never known the Lord, had their souls saved in the midst of a storm. Friend, it is God alone who can take our messes and turn them into the most beautiful of masterpieces.

Thoughts + Responses to today's study:

Day 3 – *The Best Kind of Friend*

Nothing in the world compares to the worth of a good friend. I've been fortunate enough to have a handful of them throughout my life. They are the ones who I refer to as my "middle-of-the-night-phone-call" friends; the very same ones whom I like to think I'll be drinking the perfect cup of coffee with in heaven one day. They are the ones who know my ugly side and love me still. The ones who I don't have to talk to every day or even every month, but when we are together, it's as though we've never been apart. Some of those friendships took years to form; others took me completely by surprise and happened very quickly. Both are beautiful and when I think on the faces of these women, my heart swells with gratitude that God would send friends like these into my life. I sure hope you've had a few of those types of friendships in your life. **Name a few people who come to your mind when you think of someone who has been a really good friend to you; make a note of how long you've known them.**

In the New Testament, Paul gives us a visual for the way a healthy group of believers should live life together. While he was zeroing-in on the cultural diversity between the Jewish and Gentile believers of the time, Paul still manages to teach our 21st century church about healthy, Godly relationships and how they should function.

Please read 1 Corinthians 12:14-26.

Write down verse 26 here:

Today is a lesson in friendship. And for this, we turn back to an unlikely group of men to teach us what it means to live life in tandem with others-- the sacrifice and the risk involved, but also the blessing and the beauty. The sailors on Jonah's boat may not have been aware of it, but they instinctively functioned as a body. Every part doing its best, every sailor working for the good of the whole ship, not just the good of the individual. Oh, I am praying that today we will get a fresh grasp on this notion that we really are all in this together. That when you run your race and I run mine, we can cheer one another on without feeling threatened by the success of others. That your life and my life is meant to be done alongside others and not on our own; that there is beauty in community.

Please read Jonah 1:5-16.

According to verse 6, what did the captain command Jonah to do?

Besides his being baffled that Jonah was asleep, the captain also responded with some blunt honesty: "Get up!" Listen, friend: sometimes we just need someone to remind us to *GET. UP*. To stop sleeping. To stop pouting. To alert us to what's going on around us when we are too blind to see it ourselves. To wake up, arise, and call on God. I hope we'd all be courageous enough to welcome people into our lives who care about us enough to step on our toes a little bit. I am certainly not suggesting we issue an open invitation to mean-spirited people who simply want to expose us without restoring us. Not at all. Rather, this is an encouragement to get comfortable with those who call us out in a spirit of love and redemption. **Has there ever been a time in your life a friend had to "wake you up"? Or vice versa? Has there ever been a time you've had to call out a friend?**

While the captain of the ship was not waking Jonah up because they were friends or because he felt any affection toward him at all, the captain certainly felt a sense of duty. He saw they were headed for destruction. And he felt obligated, as the captain of the ship, to warn his fellow sojourner. In the same way, can I encourage you if you see your friend on the brink of destruction, sometimes the most loving thing you can do is warn them. Do it privately and prayerfully and in a way that doesn't seek to accuse. And for heaven's sake, do it in love or don't do it at all.

Once he was confronted and after he confessed, what did Jonah tell the sailors to do to him in verse 12?

And how did the sailors respond in the very next verse?

That's amazing to me. They fought so hard for someone they hardly knew. The original Hebrew word used for "row" is literally translated "to dig." Picture that, if you will. They were digging their oars into the worst storm they had ever experienced in order to save a stranger who had just confessed to them he was the cause of the thing threatening to take their lives. They were determined not to lose this man. Why?

Rear Admiral John F. Kirby, a spokesman for the United States Pentagon, said something a few years ago which I believe applies to our sailors. "When you're in the Navy and you go overboard, it doesn't matter if you were pushed, fell or jumped, we're going to turn the ship around and pick you up."[14] Being a part of a body where every part works for the good of every other part is a beautiful thing.

The sailors did three things in an attempt to save Jonah: they woke him up, they fought their best, and what was the final thing they did according to verses 14-15?

When they could do nothing else- they handed him over to God and trusted that he knew best.

Look up Proverbs 21:30 and write it down below:

I suppose we all have times in our lives we look back on and wish we could "do-over". Times that, when we think about them, make us shake our heads and wince a little. For me, those would be the years between 12 and 16. I realize for most teenagers those are awkward years at best. But without going into too much detail, I was not only hormonal, I was also entangled in a lot of sin. I began living a sort-of "double-life" and by the time I was 16, I had lost all sense of right and wrong. I became numb to God, to his voice, and to his convictions. I pushed people away who tried to confront me and anyone who dared to disagree with me. And I got really, really good at lying. When the time came for God to deal with me, he didn't do it with a huge storm or a flash of lightning. He used a small, but solid, group of my childhood friends. I don't envy the tough call they made that summer's night so many years ago; the night they decided to call my family. The night they decided that loving me meant not covering for me. They saw the path I was on, the destruction I was headed for, and they saw how blind I was to it all. And they decided that to do what was best for me in that moment meant handing me over to the discipline, *and to the love*, of God. In so many ways, God used my friends to reroute me to him. It wasn't what I was expecting, but it was exactly what I needed.

James 5:19-20 gives us all a similar directive. I love how The Message paraphrases it:

> *"My dear friends, if you know people who have wandered off from God's truth, don't write them off. Go after them. Get them back and you will have rescued precious lives from destruction and prevented an epidemic of wandering away from God."*

At the beginning of our time today I asked you to write down any people you would consider to be some of your dearest, most impactful friends. As we conclude our study, perhaps some new names have come to mind of people throughout the years who were brave enough to be a good friend to you, even if you didn't recognize it at the time. **Take a moment and add those names to your original list.**

Now, I want to encourage you to take an action step this week. **Write a note or send an email or shoot a text to one or two of those people and express your love for them and to them.** Thank them for being a good friend to you. Even though you may very well have seen them yesterday, it never hurts to pause and let your words express what your heart feels. They may need to hear it just as much as you need to share it.

Thoughts + Responses to today's study:

Day 4- *Jonah and the Whale*

By now you will have gotten used to me asking you, almost on a daily basis, to reflect on and share bits and pieces of your personal experiences. I used to dislike it when studies asked this of me. But here's what I've learned: when I go deeper in Bible study, the Lord often brings to mind situations in my life where he's done that exact thing or something very similar. And it gets me excited! I hope by now you have sensed the excitement that comes when we remember what God has done for us. Reflecting on our stories does things to our faith; it deepens it, lengthens it, and broadens its horizons so we are filled with hope for the future. I do not want a day to go by in our study without making space for you to remember his faithfulness, wonder again at his mercies, and celebrate his goodness.

Today we have arrived at the segment of Jonah's story that is, arguably, the most famous part of the book.

Please open your Bible and read Jonah 1:17.

Despite what we've probably assumed, imagined, or even been taught our entire lives, the original Hebrew word used here is *not* whale; it is literally translated "fish." Now before we move on, here's what we are not going to do: we aren't going to get caught up on what kind of fish it was or whether or not it was actually a whale. Because, really, the fish was just a means to an end. The purpose was never to be amazed at the fact that there was a whale big enough to swallow a man whole. The purpose of the fish was always to point God. It was the second phase of God's rescue plan: he'd already gotten Jonah out of the boat with the storm. Now he was on to phase two: rescuing Jonah's life. And, as God often does, he did it in a way we wouldn't have planned or even thought possible.

Record Proverbs 16:9 below:

In your own words, what does this Scripture mean?

I have that little nugget of a verse framed and sitting near my computer at home. I glance at it often and on those days when I really take the time to let it sink in, I am overwhelmed with gratefulness that God doesn't do things my way. He does his thing, in his time, and sometimes in his own very peculiar ways.

You had to know this was coming, but here it is: **Can you think of a time in your life when you prayed for God to do something, and he did, but not at all in a way you would have expected? Please share.**

There are countless stories in the Bible we could reference which point to the miraculous, unexpected ways God intervenes for his children, but we will narrow it down to just one today. Israel's exodus from

Egypt is one of the most triumphant stories in Old Testament history and it beautifully illustrates the way God provides for us- even when we question him, fight him, and disobey him. After about 400 years in slavery, God sends Moses to bring deliverance to his people. After ten brutal plagues that ended in mass death for the Egyptian population, the Israelites are finally free of Pharaoh and their harsh slave-drivers. Or so they think.

Read Exodus 14:8-31 and answer the following questions:

How did the Israelites respond to seeing the Egyptians coming after them? (v.10-12)

What did God command Moses to do in verse 16?

According to verses 19-20, what did the angel of God and the pillar of cloud do?

Please notice something with me: how long did it take for the waters to part? (verse 21)

Do you think God could have done it quicker? Why do you think it took all night?

What happened to the Egyptians? (v. 26-28)

Where the Israelites saw no way out, God intervened. Because that's what he does. And that's who he is: our rescuer. Jonah saw no way out besides death- "throw me into the sea" – he thought his death was the price for his sin. *But God.* He rescues us in the wildest of ways sometimes. Where we see no other way, God sees the perfect way. **Record Exodus 14:14 here:**

As we wrap up our lesson today, let's come back to something we've just read and camp on it for a moment. **According to Exodus 14:8, how were the Israelites marching out of Egypt?**

The NIV says the Israelites marched out *boldly*. Oh, I love that. They didn't tuck tail and leave hoping no one would notice. They didn't try to slip under the radar. No sir. They went boldly about the thing

God was calling them to do; like it was something to celebrate and smile about. After 400 years of slavery, I think I would have been smiling too. But then something interesting happens.

At the first sign of trouble, what was their response? (verses 10-12)

Friend, I pray this is a sit-up-straight reminder for you, like it is for me, to be full of faith for the whole journey! That when God calls you out of something, he is also calling you *in* to something. That when God says go, you can be sure he *is* before you and behind you. We don't have to be bold one minute and terrified the next. You may need him to deliver you out of something, but don't forget- it's always so he can deliver you to something.

His purposes. His plans. They may be peculiar. Like a giant fish swallowing us whole – only to spit us out on the most beautiful piece of ground we've ever seen.

Thoughts + Responses to today's study:
***If you want to go deeper in today's study, you can look up the following passages of Scripture which point to the miraculous and the peculiar ways God sometimes saves his people. Take note of who the verse is about and how God provided: 1 Kings 17:2-6   John 9:1-11   Acts 12:1-11

Day 1- *A Father's Love*

Welcome to week three! Can you believe we are almost at the halfway point in our study of Jonah? Hopefully by now you are beginning to think of Jonah like an old friend – a somewhat dysfunctional, but refreshingly real, friend you can identify with on some level. After spending the better part of two weeks camped in chapter one, today we finally move on to chapter two. It's a beautiful chapter because we will hear, for the first time, Jonah talk *to* God and not just about him.

Let's briefly take a look back at Jonah 1:6-7.
What did the captain ask Jonah to do?

Based on the verses immediately following, do we have any evidence Jonah actually "called on his God" and prayed?

Now read Jonah 1:17 to Jonah 2:10.

What finally caused Jonah to pray?

We can be so stubborn, can't we? Why do we sometimes wait until we are backed into a corner before we finally call on God? When my dad was a little boy, he had been told by his mother not to climb the backyard fence. As soon as she went inside, what do you think he did? That's right. He climbed that fence and proceeded to get his leg caught in the barbwire lining the top. At this point, he obviously yelled for his mom, right? Wrong. When my dad tells the story, he says he was more scared of getting into trouble than he was scared of the blood and the pain. So he just stayed outside, stuck and hurting, for who-knows-how-long. In the midst of parenting her 7 (that's right SEVEN) other small children, my grandma eventually found my dad and when she did, she was horrified he hadn't called her for help. The barbwire went so deep into his knee that he still has scars today.

Not much changes for us as adults, by the way. When we disobey the Lord, we can get ourselves into some serious trouble. If we dig in our heels and refuse to call on him for help, we usually end up with scars that last a lifetime; scars we were never meant to have in the first place.

Somewhere between being thrown off a ship in the middle of a violet storm and then being swallowed by a giant fish, Jonah finally relented in his stubbornness and called on God.

Record Jonah 2:2 here:

Here's something we need to keep at the forefront of our minds as we read this story: just as surely as you and I are daughters of God, Jonah was a son of God. Before he was anything else, before he was a Hebrew, a prophet, or a runaway on a ship, he was simply a son who was deeply loved by his Father in Heaven. God didn't just want Jonah's obedience; he wanted Jonah's heart.

Turn to and read Luke 15:11-24.

What finally made the son in this story decide to return home? (v.17)

How did the father in this story respond to his lost son coming home?

Based on this, how then do you think God, as Jonah's father, must have felt at hearing Jonah finally call on him?

The story we've just read in Luke 15 is commonly referred to as "The Parable of the Prodigal Son." And while there is a lot of attention given to the wayward son coming back home, I would like to suggest that the focus of the story is actually the pardoning love of the father. Verse 20 describes him this way:

> *"But while (his son) was still a long way off,*
> *his father saw him and was filled with compassion for him;*
> *he ran to his son, threw his arms around him and kissed him."*

How do you think the father was able to see his son even though his son was still a long way off?

Usually, the only way I am able to see something that is far away is because *I'm looking for it*. And like the father in this story, God anticipates the return of his lost children. He is looking for them; waiting on them; ready to run to them and welcome them home.

Not only did the father see the son, but he was filled with _____.

The father didn't stand there, arms crossed, waiting for his son to make the long trek all the way up the dirt road and answer for himself. He didn't wait to offer mercy until it was asked of him. The love he had for his son compelled him to run out and meet him at the *first* sign he was on his way back home. Even in his filth, in all his rags, and in his haggard, shattered wretchedness, the Father ran and embraced his son. [15]

Likewise, God didn't wait for Jonah to get out of the giant fish and back on the road to Nineveh before he had compassion. *While Jonah was still far off*, God had mercy on him. And when Jonah cried out to him, the Lord heard him and he helped him.

And God doesn't wait for us to have our lives neatly put back together before he will accept us. He doesn't stand there, arms crossed, waiting for a really good apology from us before he'll consider welcoming us back home. *While we are still far off*, in the midst of our trouble and distress, he is looking for us. If we would but call on him, he will run to us, throw his arms around us, and welcome us back.

As we end our lesson today, choose 2 or 3 of the following Scriptures. As you read them, write down key words that describe how God cares for us as his children. I pray they encourage and remind you that you are a daughter who is greatly loved and greatly cared for by a good Father:

Psalm 139:5	**Deuteronomy 31:8**	**Psalm 68:5-6**
Matthew 6:8	**Psalm 139: 13-18**	**2 Corinthians 6:18**

Thoughts + Responses to today's study:

Day 2 –*Redemption Stories*

A few weeks ago, I was at Ikea with my two–year-old daughter when she decided it would be "fun" to play hide and seek. In the off-chance you've never been before, Ikea is basically a giant furniture warehouse that is built like a maze and can easily confuse/frustrate even the smartest of adults. It all happened so quick: one second she was holding my hand and the next she was running away to hide from me. I followed her, of course, but she darted into the next display and seemed to vanish; I couldn't see her anywhere. And then I became *that mom*- I started yelling for her, becoming slightly frantic, looking at every stranger as if they had the potential to snatch a child. We were only separated for maybe two minutes, but it was absolutely horrible; I felt sick as I looked and tried not to let the panic paralyze me. When I finally spotted her, being escorted back to me by one of the kind strangers I'd been eyeing only moments earlier, the relief swept over me. I ran to her, gave her the biggest hug and held back tears. I was not nearly as upset as I was happy to have her back.

Now it's your turn. Think of a time when you lost something valuable that you eventually found again. What was your response when you found it?

Yesterday we focused on the fact that Jonah was back. He had stopped running and was finally able to bring himself to call on God. And like a good father, the Lord was ready and waiting for his return.

Let's turn our attention now to Jonah's prayer in chapter two. Because we will be looking at this text in depth, I have included a copy of it for your convenience. It is located at the end of today's homework, on page 37. Please refer to it throughout today's study.

Before we begin, pause for a moment and try to picture Jonah inside the fish praying. As you recall the events which led up to this moment, what kind of mental and emotional state do you think Jonah was in? How do you think his prayer sounded?

As a kid, I remember seeing a movie about Jonah and he seemed completely unalarmed by the fact that he was *inside* a fish. Alive. Not being digested. He wasn't freaked out or afraid. He just kinda sat there, legs crossed, calmly looking around, as if he knew this was bound to happen. I realized recently that this early memory is something that's always stuck with me; it's how I've always pictured Jonah's redemption moment: him praying a stoic, emotionless prayer. And while the Bible is not detailed on Jonah's response to being swallowed by a giant fish, we have some clues.

Using the typed-out Scriptures on page 37, read Jonah chapter two, stopping after verse seven. Circle any verbs (action words) in those verses.

Briefly glance back at all those action words you just circled. What tense (past, present, or future) is this portion of Jonah's prayer?

Now read Jonah 2:8-9.

Did you see it? The switch from past tense to present tense? **Please note with me that verse one says he is praying from where?**

Using the clues from the text, we can reason that in the first half of Jonah's prayer, he was referencing the moments immediately following being thrown off of the boat. **Go back in the text and underline any phrases describing what Jonah experienced after he was thrown overboard.**

Based on those descriptions, how do you imagine Jonah felt at then being swallowed by a fish? Do you think he immediately saw it as God's deliverance?

I generally waver back and forth between being pessimistic and optimistic; but I think in this situation, I would have had a serious "the-glass-is-half-empty" moment. Something along the lines of "ok, this was bad, but now *this*!? I'm inside a fish?" But perhaps the moment of understanding came when he realized he'd survived; that he was alive, after not only being thrown off a boat in a crazy storm, but also after being swallowed by a fish. Either way, I don't imagine Jonah sat there calm and perfectly composed, as my childhood movie depicted, praying a stale and emotionless prayer.

According to the last sentence of Jonah 1:3, why did Jonah sail for Tarshish?

No matter the translation you are using, the message is clear: he wanted to get away from the Lord. How interesting that what he once regarded as a burden and desired to escape from, he now aches for in chapter two.

Keeping in mind everything we've studied today, I ask you the same questions I asked at the beginning of today's lesson: What kind of state do you think Jonah was in when he prayed? How do you think his prayer sounded?

We all have our own lenses through which we see and perceive things. And while all we can really do is speculate about Jonah's emotional state when he prayed, if I think about my own life experiences, I'll at least say this: at 16 years old, my redemption moment was not calm and tidy and emotionless. I didn't sit there and poetically recite a few things to God about being sorry. I was completely undone. I was crying the full-on ugly cry, the back of my throat burned from weeping so hard, my nose was running, there was a good amount of snot, and my whole body heaved and shook as I cried out to God. I literally felt the weight and the shame of my sin. And then something happened I'd never experienced before or since: I felt the almost physical-weight of my sin completely removed from me and I instantaneously felt clean. When I told my husband about it years later, I described it as "wear-white-on-my-wedding-day-clean." The ugliest moment of my life simultaneously became the most beautiful. It brings tears to my eyes every time I think about it. What an extravagant God we serve.

Jonah may not have cried the ugly cry. But I bet for the rest of his life, whenever he told his story, it caused him to remember again the foul smells and the groaning noises and the hollow darkness inside that fish; and then simultaneously remember what it felt like when God's mercy washed over him. Some of our best lessons this side of heaven are marked by our ugliest things being exchanged for beauty.

What about you? What's your redemption moment? Reflecting on our stories stirs up our faith and reminds us of what God has done for us. It causes us to celebrate again.

After you've written that part of your story, here's an action step for you to take at some point this week: share your story with somebody else. I know some of you just got really uncomfortable. But friend, the world *needs* our testimonies of God's goodness. And there is no better, and no easier place to start, than with the personal story he's written in your own life. *Only you* can tell that story.

Revelation 12:11 says defeating Satan happens through two things. Turn there now and fill in the blank:

"And they overcame him by the blood of the Lamb and _____ _____ _____ _____

_____ _____." *(NKJV)*

Our testimonies matter to a dying world that's looking for hope. As you go share your story this week remember– it might just be the redemption story somebody else needs to hear.

Thoughts + Responses to today's study:

[17]Now the Lord provided a huge fish to swallow Jonah, and Jonah was in the belly of the fish three days and three nights. [1]From inside the fish Jonah prayed to the Lord his God. [2]He said:

"In my distress I called to the Lord, and he answered me.
From deep in the realm of the dead
I called for help, and you listened to my cry.
[3]You hurled me into the depths, into the very heart of the
seas,
and the currents swirled about me; all your waves and breakers
swept over me.
[4]I said, 'I have been banished from your sight; yet I will look
again toward your holy temple.'
[5]The engulfing waters threatened me, the deep surrounded me;
seaweed was wrapped around my head.
[6]To the roots of the mountains I sank down; the earth barred me
in forever.
But you, LORD my God, brought my life up from the pit.
[7]When my life was ebbing away, I remembered you, Lord and my
prayer rose to you, to your holy temple.
[8]Those who cling to worthless idols turn away from God's love for
them.
[9]But I, with shouts of grateful praise, will sacrifice to you.
What I have vowed I will make good.
I will say, 'Salvation comes from the LORD.'"

[10]And the Lord commanded the fish, and it vomited Jonah onto dry
land.

Day 3 – *Hide These Things in Your Heart*

Although Sunday mornings are crazy in my house (hello, four kids!) I look forward to that beautiful Sabbath day each and every week. There are not many things I love more on the face of this earth than gathering together as the church. One of my favorite parts of any Sunday morning is the worship. I love that other gifted people have penned songs and hymns which seem to perfectly describe my heart toward God. As I'm writing this, I can think of several recently released worship songs that bring tears to my eyes every time I hear them; I can also recall hymns I grew up singing which still hold a dear place in my heart.

Do you have a favorite worship song or hymn?

It boils down to this: sometimes songs or poems have the ability to express exactly what we feel, we just didn't know how to put it into words. Which brings us to our man, Jonah.

We will be referring to the typed-out portion of Scripture we used yesterday, located on page 37. **Go ahead and read it (Jonah 2) now.**

Interestingly enough, most of Jonah's prayer in chapter two is actually inspired by and taken from the Psalms. Sort-of like dedicating a song to someone, the words he prayed, while he was undoubtedly sincere about them, didn't necessarily originate from him. As a Hebrew child he would have grown up learning the Psalms and committing them to memory.

Turn to and read Deuteronomy 6:4-9.

The verses we've just read are the first part of the Hebrew *Shema*. This, along with two other portions of Scripture, make up the oldest fixed daily prayer in Judaism. The Shema is recited by many Jews twice daily: once in the morning and again in the evening.

Deuteronomy 6:7 commands parents to do what?

Jonah would have been raised literally hearing these words recited morning and night; by five years old, he would have been expected to begin studying and memorizing the Scriptures. I remember being taught to memorize Bible verses from an early age. As a child, they were more words than truth to me. But this is the great mystery of Scripture: as I grew, I realized the weight of the words and the truth of them. I had unknowingly hidden God's Word in my heart and I had something firm to stand on when it mattered.

Look up the following Scriptures and list some of the additional benefits of committing God's word to memory:

Psalm 1:1-3

Psalm 119:9-11

Psalm 119:105

According to Matthew 4:1-11, when Jesus was tempted in the wilderness by Satan, how did he defeat him?

Most commentators agree that Jonah took bits and pieces from the Psalms and used them to frame his prayer. But let's not just take their word for it; let's find out for ourselves.

Look up the following verses and for each one, write down where it corresponds in Jonah's prayer from chapter two (I've done the first example for you):

Psalm 18:6 ← → Jonah 2:2

Psalm 88:6 ← →

Psalm 42:7 ← →

Psalm 31:22 ← →

Psalm 50:14 ← →

Psalm 31:6 ← →

Why do you think Jonah used the Psalms as his basis for praying rather than just creating his own prayer?

I wonder if Jonah was surprised to find these prayers rolling off his tongue. Or perhaps if, in his shock and wonder at being inside a fish, it's all he could muster up. Either way, Jonah's prayer teaches us something incredibly important: studying and memorizing Scripture matters. *It matters.*

Read Luke 6:45 and record the last sentence here:

How do you think this verse applies to Jonah's prayer?

I'm sure Jonah never thought memorizing the Psalms as a young boy would come in handy in such a physically tangible way. In referencing Jonah's prayer in chapter two, commentator Robert Jamieson says this: "Affliction opens up the mine of Scripture, before seen only on the surface."[16] Hard times reveal what we're made of, friend.

As you go on your way today, I pray you would be reminded, yet again, what we are doing on these pages isn't empty or frivolous. These times of "homework", of studying Scripture, of hearing the flipping back and forth of the thin pages in your Bible and the time spent committed to the pursuit of God…it all matters. Because a day may come when, like Jonah, you find yourself in a storm or in a dark, unfriendly place, and while your mouth may feel frozen in fear, you suddenly feel your heart burst forth with the truths you've spent a lifetime hiding there.

"Every part of Scripture is God-breathed and useful one way or another – showing us truth, exposing our rebellion, correcting our mistakes, training us to live God's way. Through the Word we are put together and shaped up for the tasks God has for us."
2 Timothy 3:16- 17 (The Message)

Thoughts + Responses to today's study:

Day 4 – *But Even If He Doesn't*

I recently bought a new Bible and was caught off guard by how emotional I got about the whole thing. I had been in the kitchen doing what moms do – making dinner and simultaneously cleaning off counters and putting away the kid's lunchboxes. So when I saw the bag with my new Bible taking up valuable counter-space, I quickly grabbed it, intending to just toss it in my bedroom. In my haste, I got a whiff of that new leather smell. I took it out of the bag and felt the smooth cover, flipped through the unmarked, unseasoned pages in front of me. It wasn't like this with my first Bible. I'd had no idea what that beautiful black leather book, now full of coffee stains and tears, would teach me. It has been my Bible through these last 15 years of marriage and it's taught me how to be a wife. Less than a year after receiving it, we lost our first baby. I'll never forget laying silently, almost unmoving, on our couch for an entire day doing one thing: reading that Bible. That's the day my trust in God began to outweigh the circumstances surrounding me. We went on to have 2 more miscarriages and 3 beautiful, healthy boys. God taught me to mother through those pages. And then at 25 years old, a fire was lit in my soul for Scripture after doing my first Bible study. That's when I finally understood people didn't just read the Bible because that's what we're supposed to do; I realized it's because we get to. Many more seasons were marked in those pages including our move to Canada and the surprise of our long prayed-for daughter. 15 years, 9 moves, 7 kids, and 2 countries; it's all these things that stirred up in me when I opened that brand-new Bible. Seeing the beauty of the unmarked pages. Knowing full-well that this new book will document new seasons, new adventures and yes- new heartbreaks. But my great joy is in knowing that the word of God and the promises of God do not change from Bible to Bible; that He is the same yesterday, today, and forever.

As we get started today, take a minute and think about your life thus far. I was able to condense part of my journey down to this: 15 years, 9 moves, 7 kids, and 2 countries. **If you had to boil your journey with the Lord down to milestone numbers, what would yours be?**

Reflection can be a beautiful thing, can't it? I know we have done a fair amount of recalling our individual stories this week, but I pray it doesn't ever get old to you. I also know it can be painful to remember certain seasons. But the beauty of life with Jesus is that, if we'll let him, he will bring purpose to our pain.

Whether you have a brand new one, or a tattered old one that's seen many years and many tears, please open up your Bible to Jonah 2 and re-read verses 2-8.

Why do you think Jonah starts his prayer off by recalling where God has delivered him from?

When we remember what God has delivered us from it helps us to step out in faith for the next leg of the journey. Not only does Jonah recall God's mercy towards him, but he goes on to do something interesting in verse nine: he stops looking backwards and starts looking forward. Unlike you and I, Jonah did not know the end of the story. He didn't know he would only be in the belly of the fish for three days. All he knew was where he'd come from and where he was currently sitting.

Keeping that in mind, read Jonah 2:9.
In your own words, what do you think Jonah is doing in this verse?

Can I confess something to you? I have a hard time with the "name-it-and-claim-it" teachings that have grown in popularity over the years. I simply do not see any Biblical evidence that says "if my faith is big enough, then _____ " and you get to fill in the blank with whatever it is you're wanting or needing. Maybe it's a raise or a new house. Or maybe it's something you're really crying out for like for your marriage to be saved or for your child to be healed. Real needs requiring real miracles. I am certainly not dismissing these needs or suggesting we shouldn't believe and trust God for a miracle. Please hear me: YES, let's believe God to work things out for us. But I have seen many people hurt, disillusioned, and disappointed because their faith in God hinged on whether or not he did the thing they were wanting.

What Jonah does in verse nine is the beautiful opposite to naming or claiming anything. I love this verse for that very reason: he simply speaks truth about who God is and how he intends to respond to that truth. And like Jonah, we must learn to position ourselves in a place where we have the faith to expect for God to meet our needs but knowing that *even if he doesn't* answer the way we want, he is still good and he is still God and he is still worthy of our trust.

Please read Daniel 3:14-27.

According to verses 17-18, how did Shadrach, Meshach and Abednego respond to the threat on their lives from King Nebuchadnezzar?

Write down the first phrase of verse 18 here:

Learning to live in the tension of the "but even if he doesn't" is where our faith gets refined.

Have you ever been bold enough to anticipate your deliverance from something without making it a crutch to your faith? In other words, have you believed God could deliver you but even if he didn't, you'd still love him no matter what?

Shadrach, Meshach, Abednego, and Jonah: every one of them believed for deliverance and things worked out in their favor, didn't it? The three men were saved from that fire just as Jonah was spit out of that fish. But what about those who pray for something, believe for something, and it doesn't happen? The deliverance doesn't seem to come?

Turn to Matthew 26:36-46 and read the account of Jesus' final moments before he is taken into custody and eventually led to the cross.

I love that we have this very personal example in the Bible. Jesus prayed something similar to "but even if he doesn't." **What was his prayer?**

How many times did he pray it?

…Yet not as I will, but as you will, Father.
…But even if you don't, Lord.

Jonah didn't know his deliverance was coming. But he positioned himself in a place where he acknowledged God's ability without demanding God's obligation.

As we come to a close on our homework this week, is there something you've been asking God for, perhaps needing a miracle for? I encourage you to write down your need below in the response section. And then end that need with "but even if you don't, Lord…" and then you fill in the blank. Take time with this. Wrestle it out with the Lord and come back to it if needed. Don't just write it and forget it. Pray it out loud and mean it. It's a hard thing to say "your will, not mine" and to hold our stuff loosely. But, friend, there's no one better to trust with every need we have. Our God is able.

> *"For the Word of the Lord holds true and everything he does is worthy of our trust."*
> *Psalm 33:4 (NLT)*

Thoughts + Responses to today's study:

Day 1- *Second Chances*

I'm no good at confrontation so I should just go ahead and tell you that today's study is going to be a work-for-it kind of day. Call me strange but I love it. I love the rustling sound my Bible makes when its pages are turned in search of something; the anticipation of finding some hidden treasure that has literally been sitting in front of me all along. I love the frayed edges of my Bible's leather binding, the coffee spots and tears that have been left on more pages than I can count – evidence that I need coffee a lot, but Jesus even more. I love the curled-up ends of those certain places where I seem to keep coming back after all these years; the ones reminding me of God's faithfulness in every season. I love seeing the things I've written over the years- the names of my kids or friends in the margins, along with prayers, longings, hopes, dreams, and plenty of heartaches. And I *love* finding Scriptures which never before held my attention, but suddenly burst onto the scene as if I've been blind all these years.

Jonah has been a burst-onto-the-scene book for me. I've learned so much already. I sure hope you have too. **As you think about what we've studied during these last 3 weeks together, what would you say is the #1 thing you've learned so far?**

Sometimes the best lessons we learn are the ones we have to labor through. **Before we begin, and to set the stage for our work today, write out Proverbs 13:4 below:**

I absolutely believe, and am trusting the Lord, that he will satisfy us today as we diligently seek him.

If you were in class, I told you as we move into chapters three and four of Jonah, we would begin to identify something in the text called chiastic structure, or chiasm. **Look back at your notes from class if you need to, but how did we define chiastic structure?**

If you weren't in class this week, please don't let this literary term scare you. To put it simply, a chiastic structure is a repetition of similar ideas in the reverse order. Did your brain just check out? I completely understand. Here, let's try this: I learn best by example, so let's look at a few fairly well-known chiasms:

You can take the girl out of the south, but you can't take the south out of the girl.

"Ask not what your country can do for you, ask what you can do for your country."[17]

"So the last shall be first, and the first last."[18]

Do you see how the ideas of the phrases are repeated, just in reverse order? It causes a mirror-effect, or a reversal, to take place. The writer of Jonah beautifully weaves chiastic structure throughout the entire book to reveal the dramatic reversals that take place. This week we will begin to un-pack these reversals because every one of them points to the main theme of Jonah: the mercy of God.

When we last saw Jonah, he was inside the belly of a fish praying.
After he prayed, what did the Lord do? (see Jonah 2:10)

Please read Jonah 3:1-3a.
Now compare those three verses to Jonah 1:1-3. What "reversal" took place in chapter 3? (In other words, rather than running, what did Jonah do instead?)

And there it is: chiastic structure; our first reversal in the book of Jonah. **How do you think this particular example points to the over-arching theme of the mercy of God?**

Go back and compare the first sentence of Jonah 1:1 to Jonah 3:1. How does the sentence change in chapter three?

Imagine it. A disobedient, runaway prophet-turned-castaway laying on a beach, covered in fish vomit, seeing the sun for the first time in three days, feeling the solid ground beneath him again. We have no way of knowing his reaction to being suddenly spit out, realizing he'd been saved, yet again, by his merciful God. He may have been wondering *what now*. He may simply have been stunned to be alive. But we do know one thing: whatever Jonah was doing, God interrupted with a second chance.

One of my family's favorite movies is *Napoleon Dynamite*, a low-budget comedy about an awkward teenage boy living with his bizarre family, including his middle-aged Uncle Rico. Throughout the entire movie, Uncle Rico laments about losing his 1982 high school championship football game. In one of the more serious lines of the movie, Uncle Rico gazes into the distance and says:

"How much you wanna make a bet I can throw a football over them mountains?... If Coach woulda put

me in fourth quarter, we would've been state champions. No doubt. No doubt in my mind. I'd have gone

pro in a heartbeat. I'd be makin' millions of dollars and livin' in a big ol' mansion somewhere."

It was a funny movie but it was a moving moment because we can probably all identify with Uncle Rico on some level. It may not be a huge, money-making, life-altering moment, but most of us wish for a do-over of some kind.

When you think back over your life, is there something you wish you could have a second chance at?

I wonder if Jonah regretted not obeying God the first time he was called. He would have saved himself so much trouble. But then again, consider how God used Jonah's disobedience.

In chapter one, how did Jonah's disobedience still eventually point to the mercy of God? (see verse 16)

How did Jonah himself experience the mercy of God? (see 1:17 and 2:10)

We may not get to go back and re-do our worst moments, but if we trust God, he uses those times for our growth and to his glory. They're never wasted. Those nights we lay our heads on our pillows thinking of all we've done or said wrong that day; those moments when we immediately know we've messed-up but we aren't sure how to fix it. These are the times Satan will try to guilt us into believing that our mistakes define us our future. But God doesn't just redeem our past; he redeems our future. He is the God of second chances. And third chances. And fourth chances. Of never-ending chances. He doesn't just save us and send us on our way. He shows up when we are covered in filth and shame on a beach somewhere and he calls us to get up again and follow him.

Well done today, my friend. I so appreciate you. As we close, look up Lamentations 3:21-23 and write it below. I pray the beauty and the truth of it would sink deep down into your heart this day.

Thoughts + Responses to today's study:

Day 2 – *Yielded Trust*

Have you ever been reading the Bible and found yourself thinking, "huh...I just don't get that?" Well, scoot over and make room for me because I'm right there with you, friend. This happens to me a lot, especially when I'm reading the Old Testament. Actually, if I'm being honest, I have "huh-I-don't-get-that" moments a lot with life in general. I don't understand wearing leggings as pants, for instance. I don't understand why man-buns are a thing or why people lose their ever-loving-minds when trying to park at Costco during the holidays. I just don't get it. But I also have some real things I'm just plain curious about; things only God can answer one day. For example: if Adam and Eve were the first humans and they only had boys, who did their sons marry? And what's the deal with dinosaurs? Did they co-exist with humans? I also have more serious questions about uncomfortable things like child abuse and human trafficking. I do not for one second believe God gets frustrated by our questions or threatened by our sincere curiosity. **Do you have any questions that, if given the chance, you'd like to ask God one day? Share them below.**

As we dig in today, feel free to ask lots of questions. Write them down, bring them to class, but most importantly: ask the Lord! Wrestling through some of this is half the fun.

Way back in week one of our homework, we learned about the city of Nineveh and the Kingdom of Assyria. **Turn to it if you need to, but try to recall from memory: why would Jonah have hesitated to go to Nineveh and preach repentance**?

Nothing has changed regarding Nineveh since the first time God called Jonah. The Ninevites are still an evil, ruthless people; they are still an enemy of Israel. But a lot has changed for Jonah. **On the timeline below, write down the major incidents that have happened to Jonah since his initial call to Nineveh in chapter one. I listed the first one.**

Jonah
runs from
God (1:3)

After all he has experienced, name 2-3 major lessons you think Jonah would have learned thus far:

Read Jonah 3:1-3. In your opinion, do you think Jonah's obedience to the Lord indicated a heart change towards the people of Nineveh? Why or why not?

Compare Jonah 1:2 to Jonah 3:2. How did God's word to Jonah change?

The first message God gave Jonah to deliver to Nineveh was specific. In chapter 3, however, it is of a more general nature. **Why do you think God would be less specific in his second instruction to Jonah?**

I tend to believe sometimes God doesn't give us the whole picture because he wants to leave some room for us to exercise our trust in him. When God called my husband and I to move our family to Vancouver 6 years ago, I initially resisted. I dug my heels in because I couldn't see how it could be good. All I saw was the financial cost and all I felt was the emotional sacrifice of leaving family and dear friends. After about a week of intense tears, prayer, and of being stripped down to bare faith, I was finally able to say, without bitterness, yes to God and no to myself. How could I have known that when we said yes to the Lord, he had our best days in front of us? I had no idea of the things to come: the miracles, the God-sized surprises, the surpassed expectations, the redemption of dreams laid down. I had no idea saying yes to God meant saying yes to all of those other things.

What about you? **Share an example of a time the Lord asked something of you that required faith.**

Let's turn our attention to someone else who was given instruction from the Lord that required tremendous trust without a full explanation.
Please read Genesis 22:1-18.

What did God command Abraham to do with his son Isaac? (v. 2)

How did Abraham respond?

If you've been in church for a long time, it can be easy to read through faith stories like this one a little too quickly, with a little too familiarity. But let's just pause for a moment and really let this sink in. Abraham was told to sacrifice, *to kill*, his only child and his response is staggering to me. He didn't argue or even ask God "why." He didn't do as Jonah did and run away or try to hide his son. His response was simple, unconditional obedience.

According to verses 16-18, how did the Lord honor Abraham's obedience? List the blessings God promised him below:

The great mystery of having faith in the Lord is trusting that *he really does know* what he's doing. Even if we can't see it or understand it. Even when it doesn't turn out the way we'd hoped or prayed for. It's not so much blind trust as it is yielded trust; we willingly trust the Lord to work all things together for his glory.

Look up Romans 8:28 and record it here:

Six years ago, I had no idea God would redeem our future; I just knew I desperately wanted to trust him. During that week of hovering somewhere between holding on and letting go, I wrote down the following from L.B. Cowman's classic devotional, *Streams in the Desert*. These words helped give form to what I was feeling at the time. Perhaps it is for some of you as well. We will end our time today with this sweet reminder that when we trust God, he doesn't just sustain us, he helps us to soar:

"The moment has come when you must get off the perch of distrust, out of the nest of seeming safety, and onto the wings of faith; just such a time as comes to the bird when it must begin to try the air. It may seem as though you must drop to the earth; so it may seem to the fledgling. It, too, may feel very like falling; but it does not fall--its pinions give it support, or, if they fail, the parent bird sweeps under and bears it upon

its wings. Even so will God bear you. Only trust Him; 'thou shalt be holden up.' 'Well, but,' you say, 'am I to cast myself upon nothing?' That is what the bird seems to have to do; but we know the air is there, and the air is not so unsubstantial as it seems. And you know the promises of God are there, and they are not unsubstantial at all. "[19]

Thoughts + Responses to today's study:

Day 3- *A Word of Warning*

When I was growing up, my grandfather had a nickname for me. Every time he'd see me, he'd say "Well hey there, Wendy!" I never asked him why he called me this, but I loved it. I always imagined the character of Wendy from *Peter Pan*, in her lovely blue dress, and kind, motherly ways. I took it as the highest form of a compliment. It wasn't until a few years ago when I finally asked about the nickname. Imagine the look on my face when my sweet 93-year old grandpa told me, *his only granddaughter*, that my nickname had never been "Wendy." It had always been "windy" – with an "i"- because when he asked me a question or I told a story, it took me a long time to get to the point. Once I got past the disillusionment of my childhood, I laughed so hard my side hurt; even now I am smiling from ear to ear. My friends who know me well are, at this exact moment, nodding their heads in approval of "windy." My sweet, and surprisingly sarcastic, grandfather was right: I love details and I find it very hard to be concise when every part of the story seems important. And, apparently, I haven't really grown out of it because my husband has now adopted the nickname for me.

Today we will look at the message Jonah delivered to the people of Nineveh. It was anything but windy; it was short and to the point. And we will see that when God's word stands alone, it can change destinies.

Please turn and read Jonah 3:1-4.

Yesterday we zeroed-in on the fact that when God called Jonah to go to Nineveh the second time, he did not give him a specific message to proclaim. **According to Jonah 3:2, what were God's exact instructions to Jonah:**

What was the message God ended-up giving to Jonah to proclaim to the people of Nineveh? (see verse 4).

Sometimes God speaks very simple messages to our hearts. But in our humanness, we can attempt to amplify his words – turning them into something he didn't intend. We forget that the weight and the worth is always in the lesson he wants to teach and no message of ours could stand up against it. Jonah seemed to realize this when he preached this short but severe message announcing Nineveh's judgement. While he may have been able to think of a more crowd-pleasing, preacher-like way to announce it, the bottom line is that God's word doesn't require our endorsement. Even when we are dying to expand on it and explain it, God's words really can stand alone. In his commentary on Jonah's announcement to Nineveh, Charles Spurgeon noted something similar:

"There is no preaching like that which Gods bids us. The preaching that comes out of our own heads will never go into other men's hearts. If we will keep to the preaching that the Lord bids us, we shall not fail in our ministry." [20]

Look up Proverbs 30:5-6 and re-write it in your own words below:

I don't know where God has you right now or what your ministry is, but don't be fooled into thinking you don't have influence. It might be your kids, it might be the other moms on the playground, it might be your co-workers, it might be your husband or your unsaved roommate, but you do have a ministry. And if you and I are ever going to be useful in God's kingdom, we've got to learn to let God do the talking for us. All we can do, all God ever asks us to do, is obey him. And he will beautifully, extraordinarily do the rest.

Flip back to Jonah and let's see how the Ninevites responded.
Read Jonah 3:5-9.

Write down the first sentence of verse 5 below:

My NIV says it very succinctly: *The Ninevites believed God.*

Before studying the book of Jonah in-depth, I would have easily read over this sentence without giving it a second glance. But this is one of those moments where our time spent in God's word makes us realize we've become students of the word. I can't read this sentence without remembering all we've learned about the Assyrians- how brutal, lethal and ruthless they were. How they worshipped many gods and hated the Israelites. And yet, in an unlikely way, from an unlikely person, the people of Nineveh not only heard the message, *they believed it*. This is another example of a reversal (or chiasm): where the Ninevites were once wicked (Jonah 1:2), they now believe in God.

Make a list below of all the things the Ninevites did as a symbol of their repentance:

According to verses 6-7, who ultimately united the people of Nineveh in repentance?

We don't know what was happening in Nineveh at the time which made the people believe and repent so readily. But could it be possible, in addition to God doing a complete miracle, it also speaks to the quality of leadership that the people were not only willing to repent, but were also prompted to repent by their King? One thing I've learned over the years is that good leaders lead by example.

What was the King's reason for commanding the national fast in verse 9?

Do we have any indication Jonah's message promised God's mercy?

There was nothing in Jonah's message that pointed to mercy. But perhaps it was the fact that God had gone to the trouble of sending a man who should have been their enemy, from hundreds of miles away, to warn them rather than just sending an army to destroy them. Maybe the warning itself was enough for them to see the vaguest possibility of mercy. And so they repented. Amazingly, their repentance was real. It was not just an emotion; it was a decision. [21]

Unlike the guilt the enemy throws at us, there will be times where we will come face to face with the Holy Spirit warning us and wanting to deal with something in our lives. When that happens, we will have to make a decision what we're going to be about. We can ignore him and keep on doing our own thing, like Jonah initially did. Or we can pay attention to the Holy Spirit's warning and, like the people of Nineveh, make a choice to literally turn away from the things entangling us. I wonder, would we be willing to do this? To not just say we're sorry, but to decide that *because* we're sorry, we will turn away from the sinful things in our lives so God can set us free.

Thoughts + Responses to today's study:

Day 4 – *Relentless Mercy*

Social Media can be the worst. "Keeping up with the Joneses" used to mean trying to keep up with your next-door neighbors, but with the dawn of Facebook and Instagram and so many other social platforms, we now have the ability to compare ourselves to people we don't even know who live halfway around the world. It's a little bit ridiculous, isn't it? But it's not all bad. I love seeing pictures and reading updates from family and friends. The trick is to stop comparing and start connecting. And every once in a while, I love social media for this very reason. I'll hop on and be unexpectedly challenged or encouraged by something I read. This happened to me a few years ago when a friend shared a story about a teachable moment with his son. It's stuck with me all these years and, with their permission, I can think of no better way to kick-off today's lesson on mercy than by sharing it with you:

My son had a TERRIBLE attitude this morning about going to school. I mean terrible. Right before we pulled up to school he said, "Dad can I have a donut?" I answered his question with a question and said, "Do you deserve a donut?" He said with a sad face, "No." To his surprise I pulled right into the donut shop and bought him one. I told him, "I'm not giving you this donut because you deserve it, I'm giving it to you because I'm good."

We've talked a lot about receiving mercy throughout our study. But today we are going to focus on those times when we are called to give mercy. Not just when we feel like giving mercy; not just when we can rationalize it or reason it. But also in those times when it doesn't make sense, when we really want the offending person to feel the heat of consequences, and yet God calls us to go against our flesh and extend grace. Let's not kid ourselves. It can be hard. It can feel wrong, like fingernails against a chalkboard. But think for a moment about those times when you've been on the receiving end. Maybe you messed up at work and you should have been fired but your boss called mercy. Maybe you should have failed that class in school but your teacher called mercy. Maybe you had an affair and your husband could have walked away but instead, he extended beautiful, redemptive mercy. When we receive it, it's like a surprise gift wrapped in sobering relief.

Outside of receiving salvation, have you ever experienced mercy when you knew you deserved far worse?

Let's try to bottle that feeling and keep it fresh before us today as we gain insights about being the ones to extend mercy.

Look up Psalm 51:17 and write it here:

According to this verse, what is it God is looking for in us?

In our study yesterday, we learned that the people of Nineveh believed Jonah but ultimately, and more importantly, they believed God and repented.

Please read Jonah 3:10.
In the space below, note how God responded to their repentance:

My NIV translation says "he relented." **In your own words, what do you think *relent* means?**

According to the Merriam-Webster dictionary, the word *relent* "implies a yielding through pity or mercy by one who holds the upper hand." [22] Although this is the first time the word has actually been used in the book of Jonah, it's not the first time it has been demonstrated. **Recall and write down instances where God has already relented and not brought about destruction within the first 3 chapters of Jonah:**

Why do you think God extended mercy to the people of Nineveh?

The Bible is full of mercy stories. One such story that comes to my mind is when Joseph forgave his brothers even after they sold him into slavery (Genesis 37-45). **Can you think of one of your favorite Bible stories about mercy? Write down a brief summary as well as its location in the Bible.** *If you are new to Bible study, read the story of Joseph in Genesis 37:23-28 and then Genesis 45:1-8:

One of my favorite books of the Bible is the curious but striking story of Hosea. It's a brilliant illustration of what God's redeeming love and mercy looks like when it's fleshed out by a human.
Turn and read Hosea 1:2-3.

What did God tell Hosea to do in verse 2?

Marry a prostitute. For any man, and a prophet no-less, this would have been a bitter pill to swallow. But Hosea obeyed and his marriage was meant to symbolize God's relationship with unfaithful Israel. After Hosea marries Gomer and they have three children, she leaves again. **Read Hosea 3:1-3.**

What did God tell Hosea to do in verse 1 of this chapter?

Love her again. If that isn't mercy, then I don't know what is. How many of us, if our husbands didn't just have an affair once, but multiple times, would go back and fight for them over and over? Think about the depth of forgiveness this requires. The depth of love. I have friends who have walked a similar road to this and I've watched them fight for their marriages, for their families, and for their future. When we choose to forgive and to turn the other cheek, it not only has mercy written all over it, it has the hand of God written all over it. And that's the thing about our God- he uses even our ugliest stuff to be worth something because it points back to him every.single.time. We may not get to see its full worth this side of heaven but don't mistake your pain to be purposeless.

The rest of Hosea is filled with both charges against unfaithful Israel (represented by Hosea's wife, Gomer) and promises of restoration. **Read Hosea 2:14-23 and write down verse 15 below:**

The valley of trouble into a gateway of hope. Pause for a second and think about that person or those people in your life to whom you've admittedly struggled to show mercy. Think of their faces. Please hear this, friend: could it be that God wants to use you in that person's life to turn a valley of trouble into a gateway of hope? Don't think I'm suggesting you stay in an unhealthy, abusive or destructive relationship; forgiveness is not the equivalent of reconciliation. But I am saying that maybe the best thing we can do for people who hurt us is to let go of our anger and our frustration and allow our mercy to give way to hope in their lives, and freedom in ours.

As we wrap up our week, **think about one action step you can take in the next few days** to display mercy to one of the people on your list. Maybe it's to pray for them more. Maybe it's nothing tangible at all and you are simply going to decide that rather than letting the root of bitterness grow when you think about them, you'll commit to stop those thoughts in their tracks. **Whatever you decide, write it here:**

I have probably had more mercy moments with my kids than with anyone else. As happy as my kids are in those times when they receive mercy, as their mom, it gives me even greater joy to see their response; to see the startled relief flood their faces, and to feel the warm bear-hug as they realize they aren't getting what they deserve. Although, admittedly, I sometimes wonder "did they even learn anything?" I've also learned to trust God, knowing sometimes mercy can teach just as strong a lesson as discipline.

The most beautiful part about the book of Hosea is that we see God going after his people over and over. That's really what the book of Jonah is about too. Then again, this is what the whole Bible is about, isn't it? The entire God-story is about him pursuing us, rescuing us, redeeming us, and showing us undeserved, relentless mercy.

Well done, friends. See you in class.

Thoughts + Responses to today's study:

Day 1 – *Reaping and Sowing*

Discipline. It's not a nice-sounding word, is it? Until my husband and I had kids, it wasn't something we regularly thought about. But now that we are in the thick of raising four children ranging in ages from 2 to 12, it's a word that is used on a regular basis in our house. I take comfort in knowing it's something every generation of parents has had to face. I get a kick out of it when I hear stories about the creative ways parents have tried to effectively discipline their kids – things ranging from time-outs, to doing chores, to being grounded, to working in the yard. I know a lovely senior woman who had NINE boys (*yes, she deserves a medal of some kind*) and when I asked her how in the world she did it, she said, with a twinkle in her eye I might add, "Oh honey. I locked them outside after they'd get home from school. They weren't allowed in until dinner time. If they fought, they had to figure it out with one another." I tried that with my own boys, by the way, and it was an epic failure. I heard another story about a woman with six boys who made them run laps around the house at night if they wouldn't settle in for bedtime. I tried that too and it completely backfired- not only were my boys not tired, the running woke them up even more. The older the generation, the more intense the discipline seemed to be. My parents had to choose thin branches off of trees in their backyards for their swats and my grandparents were spanked with belts. I even know one woman who wasn't allowed to shave her legs until high school because of disobedience to her parents and do you know what? She wasn't scarred for life; in fact, she laughs every time she tells the story. Because really, parents of every generation are just trying to do what's best for our kids, aren't we? We all experience parenting fails and we mess up and make mistakes and hopefully, in the midst of tears, we are able to have some laughter along the way.

How do you feel about discipline? Does it strike up negative or positive thoughts in your head? (please note: we are not necessarily addressing corporal punishment here, but consequences for a wrong that's been done).

The more we get to know God, the more we realize that he often doesn't discipline the way we think he should. Jonah certainly felt this way when God had mercy on the people of Nineveh. At the end of our time together last week, we learned how God relented and did not carry out the destruction he'd originally threatened.

Read Jonah 4:1-4.

What was Jonah's complaint?

And so after all these weeks of study, we learn Jonah's real reason for running from God in the first place. **What did he say his reason was?**

We have to give credit to Jonah for at least phrasing his complaint against God brilliantly. He simultaneously complained and complimented him. *Oh Jonah.* If you'll remember from our time studying his prayer in chapter two, Jonah grew up memorizing Scripture, including the Psalms. **Turn and read Psalm 86:15 and compare it Jonah 4:2. Write down any descriptive words that are the same in both verses:**

In week three of our homework, we read the story of the prodigal son. At the time, we focused on the lost son and the father who welcomed him home. But there is one more character in this story who is worthy of our attention.

Turn and read Luke 15:11-31 and answer the following questions:

How did the older brother respond to his little brother's celebrated homecoming? (v. 28-29)

According to verse 32, why did the father say they had to celebrate?

Do you notice any resemblance in behavior between the older brother and Jonah?

Both men responded in anger. What's more is that they both felt as if a reckoning hadn't taken place; the older brother wanted to see his little brother pay the cost for his recklessness and Jonah wanted to see the sins of the Ninevites come back on them. They didn't feel that proper discipline had been carried out.

Has there been a time when you were troubled by someone who seemingly "got away" with something that was wrong?

Let's be honest: sometimes we want a public shaming when God wants a private correction. We want to know so-and-so was dealt with or is going to be punished for something that was done. If you're like me, then you will understand some of Jonah and the older brother's feelings because I definitely lean more towards the justice side of life than the mercy side. I tend to want to see that the price has been paid. Because of this, it can be easy to read these accounts about the people of Nineveh and the prodigal son and determine all we have to do to avoid God's discipline is repent. But if this is the conclusion we come to, we are sorely missing a huge piece of the puzzle. **Look up Galatians 6:7 and write it here:**

God's definition of discipline is not the same as ours. He is a God of seasons and so we must remember: for everything that is planted, there is a natural reaping. While the people of Nineveh experienced the miraculous mercy of a good God and avoided destruction, they still had to wake up the next day and bear the consequences of their sins; they had to learn what it meant to live life in a radically different way than they ever had before. It wouldn't have been easy. Let's not assume that because they avoided death, they somehow got away with something.

Look up 1 Samuel 16:7 and write down the last sentence of that verse.

Only God knows what's going on inside of our hearts. And when we feel justice isn't being served, we must remember we have no idea what God is doing in that person privately or how he is dealing with them behind closed doors. The Lord reserves the right to do things his own way because it's always the most effective way.

A few weeks ago, I shared a part of my personal testimony- that moment when I felt the forgiveness and grace of Jesus wash over me from head to toe. But don't for one moment think it was all sunshine and roses after that. I still had to bear the consequences of my sin for well over another year – in fact, some things were carried into my marriage which my husband and I had to walk through. I learned that while God's forgiveness redeems us, it doesn't instantly undo what's already been done. Because he's good, because he wants us to learn and to grow, God allows us to reap what we've sown. And while it isn't always fun, you can be sure it will always be fruitful.

Thoughts + Responses to today's study:

Day 2- *Anger Management*

I have a running joke with some of my girlfriends where we admit we never knew we had anger issues until we had kids. We are KIDDING, of course, but c'mon fellow moms...you can at least understand where we're coming from, can't you? It's the little things kids do that we never knew could bother us in such irrational ways. Things like forgetting to flush the toilet (if you're a boy mom and you've mastered teaching your kids this lost art, I'm going to ask you to put this book down and email me ASAP; I need your help). It's the toothpaste that mysteriously ends up on the mirrors and the Lego pieces that end up in the bottom of my bare foot at 5 am while I'm holding my hot coffee. I'm laughing right now but if I'm being honest with you, I rarely laugh in the heat of the moment. It has very little to do with my kids and much more to do with me. These kinds of things, while funny to laugh at, can actually irritate to the point of frustration which, in my case anyway, can easily lend itself to turning into full-blown anger. Did you catch that progression? What begins as irritation, if not dealt with, evolves into frustration and crescendos into anger. It's so silly and it's one of those things about myself that I really dislike. But you'll be happy to know that the Lord is working on me in this area. If you're anything like me, then today is for us, friend. Come, let's go through some anger management together.

During the last several days of homework, we have seen a string of responses to the events that have unfolded. Let's backtrack a little and connect some dots. **In each of the following instances, record what the response was, using as little as 1 -2 words:**

Jonah 2:9   **Jonah's response to God's saving mercy on him:**

Jonah 2:10- 3:1-2   **God's response to Jonah's prayer:**

Jonah 3:5-9   **Nineveh's response to God's warning:**

Jonah 3:10   **God's response to Nineveh's repentance:**

Jonah 4:1-3   **Jonah's initial response to God's mercy on Nineveh:**

Now turn and read Jonah 4:1-11.

What did Jonah do in verse 5?

Why are Jonah's actions here ironic? Do you see a reversal between his attitude in chapter two and now?

One word comes to my mind: *stubborn*. Jonah already knew God had made a decision regarding Nineveh and had chosen to relent. **So why in the world do you think Jonah decided to go sit, watch and wait to see if the Lord would still overthrow Nineveh? What do you think this says about Jonah's character?**

I don't know about you, but there have been times in my life where I've disagreed with God. Where something has happened and I just flat out didn't like it. But, you know, I think he's ok with that. Because he's not threatened by us when we disagree or get mad about one of his decisions; he doesn't think to himself *well maybe that was a mistake*. No, I believe he's ok with our disagreement as long as we are still able to walk in obedience; when our hearts are able to walk in the tension of not understanding the full picture but still trusting God with the outcome.

Has there ever been a time when you admittedly disagreed with God? If you're taking the class and you'd be willing to share this week, we would love it. Remember our stories can prompt others into obedience and faith!

Jonah's actions in verse five suggest he not only disagreed with God's decision, but he was still persisting in his expectancy and his desire to see the people of Nineveh destroyed.

What lesson do you think God was trying to teach Jonah through the plant in verses 6-11?

How did Jonah respond to the life and death of the plant?

It's hard to be merciful toward others when we are clouded with anger. Anger does this to us, doesn't it? It blinds us and causes us to overreact; our selfishness erupts and our immaturity gets magnified.

How many times did Jonah wish for death in chapter 4? _____

Turn and read James 1:19-20.

According to these verses, there are two things we can do which will result in dealing with anger the right way. Think of this like a flow chart or step-by-step directions. **Fill in the following blanks according to James 1:19:**

1. Be quick to _____.

Step #1 in dealing with anger? Listen. A lot. Are you quick to listen? Not just to the Lord; but to other people. To your friends, your co-workers, your family. Let's not rush through this. Please pause and really consider: are you a good listener? My husband is an amazing listener, bless his heart. And I will be the first to admit I have a tendency to try to fill awkward silence with words (do you remember how my grandfather used to call me Windy?). But a sign of maturity in Christ is learning how to listen. Proverbs 1:5 says, "let the wise listen." And then once we have listened....

2. Be slow to _____.

Being slow to speak doesn't mean we don't speak at all. It means that when we do speak, our words aren't just spit out, but rather that they are intentional. Rather than reacting, we are able to respond. Proverbs 18:13 in The Message cuts to the heart of it: "Answering before listening is both stupid and rude." Listening enables us to speak rationally.

Like a flow chart, if we do both of these things – if we are quick to listen and slow to speak – we will be much more equipped to do the third thing:

3. Be slow to _____.

Read the following verses and write down the consequences of unbridled anger:

Psalm 37:8

Proverbs 15:18

Proverbs 29:22

Ephesians 4:26

As we become mature believers in Christ, we have to start asking ourselves some tough questions. And so, as we end today, I am going to ask you to do a bit of homework. You can do it now as your wrap-up, or you can do it on your own time. But I believe it's an important self-evaluation we all need to consider.

Turn to Galatians 5:19-26. In it you will find two lists: one list is made-up of things that are identified as being "acts of the flesh" and the second list is the "fruit of the spirit." On the following page, you will find two blank columns. Write down the attributes listed in Galatians 5 in the appropriate columns. And then pray. Are there things in the flesh you see in yourself? Are there things God wants to replace with the fruit of his spirit? Because the truth is, he doesn't just want us to learn how to manage our anger; he actually wants to replace it with his always kind, never-selfish, overly-generous love.

Well done, my friend. Only 2 more days together. See you tomorrow.

Thoughts + Responses to today's study:

Galatians 5:19-26

Acts of the Flesh

Fruits of the Spirit

Day 3 – *But God*

Ravi Zacharias was born into a Hindu family in India in 1946. He longed to become a professional cricketer, but he performed miserably in school. In India, this was a formula for failure. According to Ravi, "Indian children are raised to live with books and get to the top of the class, or else face failure and shame." As a result, Ravi's father would humiliate and beat him. At the age of 17, Ravi attempted to commit suicide in order to save his family from further shame. *But God.* He was immediately rushed to the emergency room. It was while lying in the hospital that a Youth for Christ director brought Ravi a Bible and told him to read John 14. Five days after being wheeled into the ER, Ravi left the hospital a changed person. Today Ravi is a Christian apologist, preaching in more than 70 countries, including the campuses of some of the world's leading universities. [23] He has written over 25 books in the fields of theology, apologetics, comparative religion, and philosophy. He and his wife have been married 45 years and have 3 kids. [24]

My husband's grandfather was on his deathbed with terminal cancer in 1965. *But God*. He was miraculously healed and went on to live another thirty-four years, entirely cancer-free, telling anyone who would listen about God's healing hand.

At 6 months pregnant, my mom was being prepared for surgery to remove her baby because of a severe case of placenta previa. *But God*. He intervened and my mom gave birth to me 3 months later.

You and I may not have stories as dramatic as these, but don't think we haven't had our own "but God" moments. They happen all the time if we would but learn to recognize them.

Have you had a "But God" moment recently? Please share:

Refer back to Jonah 1:3 and fill in the following blanks:

"_____ _____ ran away..."

At the end of week one, we went into depth on those times when, like Jonah, you may have had moments when you felt the Lord prompt you to do something but instead, you did something else. It happens to all of us because none of us are perfect. But today we turn our attention to how God willingly steps in to teach us when we get caught up in doing things our own way.

Jonah has another "but" moment God addresses in chapter 4.
Look up Jonah 4:1 and write it down below:

Read Jonah 4:4-11 and take note of every time the phrase "But God" occurs. How many times does it happen?

In each of these instances, we see God step-in to address Jonah's lack of compassion for the people of Nineveh. How strange that Jonah, who has experienced abundant mercy himself, is so quick to withhold it. What about us? When we read the Bible, we must continually ask ourselves: what is it God is trying to teach me? Perhaps we all, like Jonah, need the lesson taught in the parable of the unforgiving, though forgiven, debtor. **Let's turn and read this story now in Matthew 18:21-35.**

Write down verse 33 here:

We have had people on our hearts and minds throughout this study whom we have been struggling with. Some of us have been horribly abused and have faced desperate situations. Please hear me when I say I do not want to minimize this fact. But I have to believe that the Word of God applies to every situation, including those who have faced the unimaginable.

The parable Jesus tells in Matthew 18 is a response to a question Peter asks in verse 21. What was the question? (see Matthew 18:21)

I love this question because it acknowledges that people do hurt us; that we are wronged and sinned against. But in true Christ-like fashion, the parable Jesus tells doesn't address those who did the wrong; instead Jesus zeroes-in on Peter's response to those who hurt him. Ultimately God is much more concerned about the condition of our hearts than he is concerned about whether or not we feel justified. If we are so busy making sure everyone around us is getting what they deserve, not only does it rob God from being the ultimate authority and judge in our lives, it also distracts us from being effective in our time here on earth. **Look up the following Scriptures and record them below:**

Psalm 75:7

Romans 12:19

How freeing to know that God does not miss a thing. He sees it all. The Lord never minimizes our hurts; but he always maximizes the need for forgiveness. Listen, friend. If you are having a hard time letting go of something someone did to you- perhaps as a child or even in more recent years, I want to encourage you that God knows. *He knows.* And he hasn't forgotten you. Vengeance is his. Trust him with it. Trust him to rightly judge what's been done to you and against you. As we said a few days ago, forgiveness does not mean reconciliation must automatically take place. There will be fences God does not ask you to mend and relationships he does not ask you to reunite with. Forgiveness has the ability to function apart from the need for reconciliation because it only requires *your* cooperation; no one else's. When it comes to our view of those who have hurt us, God is much more concerned with our response: will we choose forgiveness? Will we choose mercy? The condition of our hearts shapes our effectiveness here on earth and ultimately, it has eternal consequences.

Even from the beginning of time, we see "but God" moments taking place.

Turn and read Genesis 3:6-8.

Before Adam and Eve sinned, they were living in a perfect, completely balanced and peace-filled world. Imagine that! No hunger or poverty. No unmet needs. No war or hatred. Everything was perfectly orchestrated day-after-day. And then in an instant, sin arrived. **Read Genesis 3:9 and note how God responds to their sin:**

There it is again. *But God.* He called out to them. He didn't abandon them or throw up his hands in frustration at how quickly they fell into sin. There were consequences they had to face; in fact, every generation since has had to face the same consequences: death. But even then, God put a plan into place to save us. The following portion of Romans 5, taken from The Message, is a fitting description of how God went on to have his ultimate "but God" moment:

"You know the story of how Adam landed us in the dilemma we're in—first sin, then death, and no one exempt from either sin or death. That sin disturbed relations with God in everything and everyone... But Adam, who got us into this, also points ahead to the One who will get us out of it... Here it is in a nutshell: Just as one person did it wrong and got us in all this trouble with sin and death, another person did it right and got us out of it. But more than just getting us out of trouble, he (Jesus Christ) got us into life! One man said no to God and put many people in the wrong; one man said yes to God and put many in the right." (Romans 5:12;18-19)

Adam sinned.
But God.
Death created an abyss that separated us.
But God.
We sin and we fall short.
But God.

If we walk away from our time studying this book and learn nothing else, please learn this: *God is all about people*. He always has been and always will be. He has stepped in throughout the course of history for the sake of his people. He has corrected the mistakes of mankind over and over again. And we see him step in throughout the Bible to remind us that he's not plan B; he's always been plan A. And every time he has to intervene and draw us back it's not because his plan failed; it's because we failed. *But God*. We may fail, but because of him, we are not failures. And it's because he is so completely and absolutely committed to us and his love for us, that he looks on us with compassion and mercy and his love for us outweighs his anger against us.

> *"But God, being rich in mercy, because of the great love with which he loved us,*
> *even when we were dead in our trespasses,*
> *made us alive together with Christ—by grace you have been saved."*
> *Ephesians 2:4-5 (ESV)*

But God. Some of the sweetest words we will ever hear.

Thoughts + Responses to today's study:

Day 4 – *Something Greater Than Jonah*

I hate goodbyes. I really do. I get super awkward and I usually try to crack some kind of joke that inevitably falls flat. I guess I'm hoping humor will somehow act like a Band-Aid and keep the pain from spilling out. It can be so hard saying goodbye. But it's also necessary, isn't it? Letting go of one season and leaning into the beauty of the next is how we grow up and move forward in our faith. And so today as we come to a close on our time together, I am trusting that as the Lord closes one chapter, he is opening up a new one in your life.

Now come, let's sit at the feet of Jesus together one more time, and learn our final lesson. I promise I'll try to steer clear of bad jokes and awkward tears.

We knew when we started this study that the book of Jonah leaves us with an-open ended question; it leaves us with a decision about how we are going to live our lives. A question that ultimately asks us: what, or more importantly *who*, are we going to be about?

Please turn in your Bibles and read Matthew 12:38-39.

According to verse 38, what did the Pharisees ask for?

Jesus' response in verse 39 was bold, wasn't it? I mean, think of the last time you called someone in church "wicked and adulterous" to their face. I'm guessing you probably never have. And if you're like me, you might wonder why Jesus responded so passionately to their seemingly innocent question. It's not as if people in the Bible hadn't asked for signs before: Gideon asked for a sign in Judges 6; Hezekiah asked for a sign in 2 Kings 20; and several others asked for signs, as well.

Fast-forward for a moment to Matthew 23:1-7. As you read these verses, take note below of the ways Jesus describes the Pharisees:

If this doesn't make the hair on the back of your neck stand-up, please read it again. In fact, if you continue reading the rest of the chapter, it only gets more intense. The description Jesus gives of the Pharisees sounds eerily close to our generation, doesn't it? **In what ways, if any, do you think the Pharisees sound similar to our current Christian culture?**

We live in a culture right now, and I am talking about a *Christian culture*, where everyone seems to want a platform. Self-promotion has infiltrated the church in mass quantity and it is erasing humility from among us. I find myself raising my children among a selfie-generation, and I'm not necessarily talking about pictures. Selflessness has been set to the side while Christians are simultaneously craving the honor, attention, and I daresay the approval, of this world. *Heaven help us.*

But as for us.

Friends. *Sisters.* I pray that as for us, as for our households, we would have the courage and the conviction to be different than so many in our generation. I pray we would be so enthralled and fulfilled by the scope of God's love that we'd be just fine to live our lives off the world stage, not craving the approval of man. That we would be completely satisfied serving our God and serving one another in humility. I also pray we wouldn't hide behind our faith, but, as David Platt wrote, "may it be said of us that we not only held firm *to* the gospel, but that we spoke clearly *with* the gospel to the most pressing issues of our day."[25] That unlike the Pharisees, you'd practice what you preach and indeed, that *your very life* would preach the greatest sermon ever told to the people around you.

When the Pharisees asked for a sign in Matthew 12, Jesus wasn't being rude to them; he simply wasn't willing to have to prove himself to people who were already determined not to believe in him. And though Christ is always ready to hear and answer Godly desires and prayers, signs throughout the Bible were granted to those who desired them to *confirm their faith*; but signs were denied to those who demanded them to *excuse their unbelief.*[26]

Go ahead and turn back to Matthew 12 and read verses 39 through 41.

Fill in the following blanks according to the last section of verse 41:

"…for they repented at the preaching of Jonah, and now _____ _____ _____ _____ is here."

What is the "something greater" Jesus is referring to?

Why do you think Jesus compared himself to Jonah? Note any similarities and differences.

If you were to google "Jesus and Jonah," you would get a thousand different links to a thousand different thoughts on why Jesus connected himself to the likes of Jonah. Theologians have written volumes of commentaries on it and Pastors have preached all kinds of sermons on it. And while there are so many good, worthwhile reasons to discuss why Jesus is the "something greater than Jonah," today we will end our 5-week journey together by narrowing it down to only one reason: *while they both preached a message of the coming judgement, Jesus took it a step further and also preached redemption.* Jesus didn't just tell us what was going to happen to us, he also offered us a way out: himself.

In Matthew 12:40, what example does Jesus first use to compare himself to Jonah?

Refer back to Jonah 1 if you need to, but try to recall from memory: why was Jonah in the belly of the fish in the first place?

Jonah ran, hid and ultimately disobeyed. It was his very own sin which landed him in the belly of that fish.

Look up 2 Corinthians 5:21 and write it down below:

Unlike Jonah's time in the fish, Jesus was not in the grave because of his sin. He was in the grave because of *our* sin. Yours and mine.

Let's look at John 5:24. What did Jesus say about those who believe in him?

Unlike Jonah, who preached judgement and had the heart of a judge, Jesus preached judgement and had the heart of a redeemer.

Look up 1 John 3:16. What command are we given?

Unlike Jonah, who was angry enough to die because of God's grace toward sinners, Jesus was compassionate enough to die because of his love for sinners. *Jesus is the better Jonah.*

Please turn one last time to the book of Jonah and look up the very last verse (4:11).

And therein lies the question before us, friend: What are we going to be about? Whose example will we follow? Will we, like Jonah, refuse to offer forgiveness and mercy and compassion? Or will we, like, Jesus, choose love? Will we remember how much mercy we, ourselves, have experienced? Will we choose to lay down our lives for those around us; to stop being selfish, like the Pharisees were and like so many in our generation are becoming, and start being selfless?

I pray during our time together you've learned much, gained new insights, and had some of your old ways of thinking threatened in the best way by the truth of the gospel. I pray you've fallen even deeper in love with this God of ours. And finally, I sincerely hope if you didn't love studying God's Word before, that a new fire was lit in your soul. My hope for all of us on this journey is to remind us that studying God's Word isn't homework; it's like coming home. He is worth every second of our time.

And now, as you close this book and get up from that chair, I challenge you to decide for yourself what you are going to be about. I believe it is entirely possible that we can link arms, across denominations and generations, and go be women defined by our love for God, his Word, and for all people. Friend, let's go change our world.

"So this is my prayer: that you will flourish and that you will not only love much but well...live a life Jesus will be proud of: bountiful in fruits from the soul, making Jesus Christ attractive to all, getting everyone involved in the glory and the praise of God." (Philippians 1:9;11 MSG)

Thoughts + Responses to today's study:

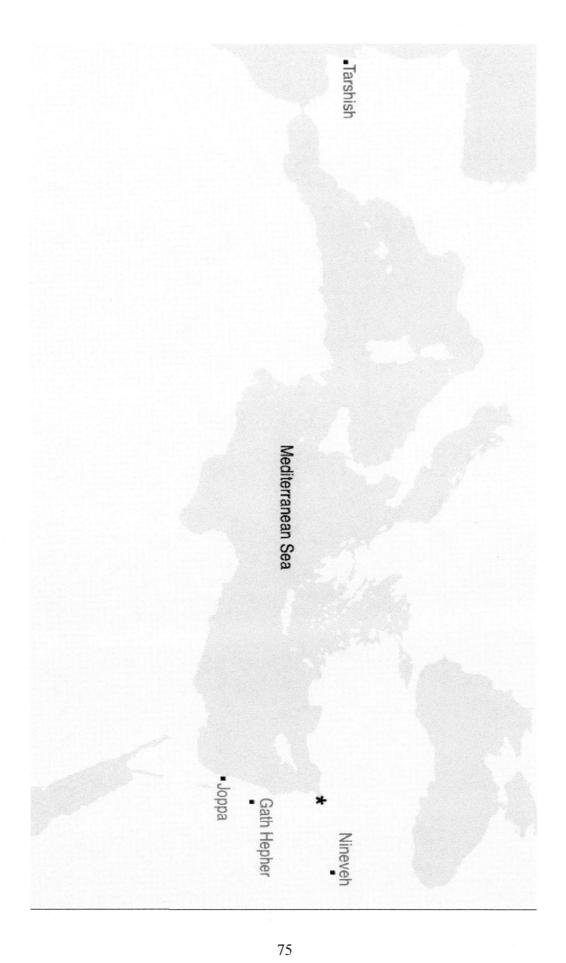

About the Author

Elita is a proud Texan living in Canada with Ryan, her husband of 15 years, and their four wild but wonderful young kids: Noah, Jackson, Seth, and Macy Jo. In 2006, she graduated from the University of Mobile (Alabama) with a Bachelor's degree in Communication and a minor in Worship Leadership.

In 2011, Elita and her family re-located from Alabama to a suburb of Vancouver, British Columbia. She is currently a stay-at-home-mom, has miraculously avoided driving a minivan, and her kids are happy to report she no longer homeschools. Some of Elita's favorite things include strong coffee, dear friends, good food and spontaneous adventures.

Elita and her family attend Christian Life Assembly in Langley, British Columbia, where she serves as the volunteer director for a weekly women's program, *Mornings With Her.* She finds it a joy and an honor to regularly teach and serve women at these events.

Elita has been described as encouraging, humorous, and relevant. As a teacher and writer, she has a deep desire to see women of all ages, and in all stages of life, become biblically literate. Her passion is for women not just to read God's Word, but to love it and live it. Elita believes it is entirely possible to encounter Jesus from your living room couch while flipping through a coffee-stained, tear-filled Bible that has been colored on and scribbled in by toddlers. That's her story and she wouldn't have it any other way.

Because she really likes being a wife and mom, Elita is a sometimes writer, sometimes blogger, sometimes Instagrammer. You can find her here:

www.elitafriesen.com
www.thefriesenfive.blogspot.com
@elitafriesen

[1] *The Names of God in the Old Testament* (n.d.) Retrieved September 3, 2017 from https://www.blueletterbible.org/study/misc/name_god.cfm

[2] *Laughing Dove Streptopelia senagalensis.* (n.d.) Retrieved September 14, 2017. from http://www.oiseaux-birds.com/card-laughing-dove.html

[3] *Nesting Habits of Doves.* (n.d.) Retrieved September 14, 2017 from http://animals.mom.me/nesting-habits-doves-6319.html

[4] D.W.B. Robinson, *The New Bible Commentary: Revised*, 1967, p.746.

[5] James Strong, *The New Strong's Exhaustive Concordance of the Bible.* Nashville: Thomas Nelson Publishers, 1984.

[6] Enrique Baez, "Nimrod, Son of Cush," ed. John D. Barry et al., *The Lexham Bible Dictionary* (Bellingham, WA: Lexham Press, 2016) emphasis mine.

[7] D.D. Lowery, "Assyria" ed. John D. Barry, et al., *The Lexham Bible Dictionary* (Bellingham, WA: Lexham Press, 2016).

[8] Anna Sieges, "Nineveh" ed. John D. Barry et al., *The Lexham Bible Dictionary* (Bellingham, WA: Lexham Press, 2016).

[9] Albert Kirk Grayson, *Assyrian Royal Inscriptions, Part 2: From Tiglath-pileseri to Ashur-nasir-apli II* (Wiesbaden, Germ.: Otto Harrassowitz, 1976), 143.

[10] Daniel David Luckenbill, *Ancient Records of Assyria and Babylonia*, 2 vols. (Chicago Univ. of Chicago Press, 1926-1927), vol. 1, secs. 584-585; 599.

[11] Matthew Henry, "Jonah". *Matthew Henry Commentary on the Whole Bible (Complete)*, 1706. N.P. Accessed November 19.2017. https://www.biblestudytools.com/commentaries/matthew-henry-complete/jonah/1.html

[12] Ibid.

[13] John D. Barry, Douglas Mangum, Derek R. Brown, et al., *Faithlife Study Bible* (Bellingham, WA: Lexham Press, 2012, 2016), Jon 1:5.

[14] Eric Schmitt, Helene Cooper and Charlie Savage, "Bowe Bergdahl's Vanishing Before Capture Angered His Unit." *The New York Times*, June 2, 2014. Accessed November 28, 2017. https://www.nytimes.com/2014/06/03/us/us-soldier-srgt-bowe-bergdahl-of-idaho-pow-vanished-angered-his-unit.html

[15] Robert Jamieson, A. R. Fausset, and David Brown, *Commentary Critical and Explanatory on the Whole Bible*, vol. 2 (Oak Harbor, WA: Logos Research Systems, Inc., 1997), 115.

[16] Robert Jamieson, A. R. Fausset, and David Brown, *Commentary Critical and Explanatory on the Whole Bible*, vol. 1 (Oak Harbor, WA: Logos Research Systems, Inc., 1997), 684.

[17] John F. Kennedy's Inaugural Address, Jan. 20, 1961

[18] Matthew 20:16 (KJV)

[19] L.B. Cowman, *Streams in the Desert 21st Ed.* (The Oriental Missionary Society, 1941), 207.

[20] Charles Spurgeon, "Commentary on Jonah 3:4". *Spurgeon's Verse Expositions of the Bible.* Retrieved December 11, 2017. https://www.studylight.org/commentaries/spe/jonah-3.html. 2011.

[21] Eugene Peterson, *A Long Obedience in the Same Direction.* (Intervarsity Press, 1980, 2000), 29.

[22] Relent. 2018. In *Merriam-Webster.com.* Retrieved January 3, 2018 from https://www.merriam-webster.com/dictionary/relent

[23] Ravi Zacharias, "Antidote to Poison." *Christianity Today*, April 26, 2013. Accessed January 5, 2018. http://www.christianitytoday.com/ct/2013/april/antidote-to-poison.html

[24] Ravi Zacharias International Ministries. Accessed January 6, 2018. http://rzim.org/about/ravi-zacharias/

[25] David Platt, *Counter Culture* (Carol Stream, IL: Tyndale, 2015), 19.

[26] Matthew Henry's Bible Commentary, emphasis mine.

Made in the USA
Middletown, DE
25 April 2023

29034050R00046